THE .4XTEA

TRADER'S MANUAL

THE MANDATORY GUIDE TO SUCCESSFUL FOREIGN EXCHANGE TRADING

.4xTeam

Jonas Navardauskas

Jonas Navardauskas
Owner of .4x Team

Our content is intended to be used and must be used for informational purposes only. It is very important to do your own analysis before making any investment based on your own personal circumstances. You should take independent financial advice from a professional in connection with, or independently research and verify, any information that you find on our Website and wish to rely upon, whether for the purpose of making an investment decision or otherwise.

Futures, stocks and options trading involves substantial risk of loss and is not suitable for every investor. The valuation of futures, stocks and options may fluctuate, and, as a result, clients may lose more than their original investment. The impact of seasonal and geopolitical events is already factored into market prices. The highly leveraged nature of futures trading means that small market movements will have a great impact on your trading account and this can work against you, leading to large losses or can work for you, leading to large gains.

If the market moves against you, you may sustain a total loss greater than the amount you deposited into your account. You are responsible for all the risks and financial resources you use and for the chosen trading system.

Jonas Navardauskas
.4x Team
www.4xteam.co.uk
United Kingdom

Publication date: 11/01/2020
Imprint: Independently published (.4x Team)
ISBN: 9781659047172

Financial charts have been obtained from uk.tradingview.com

Jonas Navardauskas
Owner of .4x Team

Jonas Navardauskas
Owner of .4x Team

Introduction

It's unfortunate that up to 95% of all traders begin with no trading experience - lose large amounts of money and give up. Considering the fact that trading the foreign exchange markets can make anybody a ridiculous amount of money, I never understood people that quit.

The earning potential from trading financial instruments such as the foreign exchange and indices market is astonishing and ensured that I constantly worked on myself to become a better trader, daily, for the past four years - I hope that is the same mindset that you've come into this manual with.

It is vital that trading is explained to you in the correct manner. Forex is undoubtedly the largest market in the world, with over $5.1 trillion being exchanged daily, of which it is easier than ever to participate in due to the Internet threatening the online trading event. There are tens of thousands of social media "Forex professionals" who have barely experienced the potential of the markets but are already selling signals, robots or private-access blogs "guaranteeing" you profit every single trade.

Profitable trading is only for a select few, and expectations cannot rule over the reality of trading.

This book needs to be used as a trading manual that you have access to at all times during trading sessions due to the availability of being able to recap specific patterns to ensure that the market conditions suit the pattern wanted.

There are multiple factors barriering many traders from being successful. Uncertainty, fear and greed are some of them - but the largest one by far is lack of education.

If you lack education in the forex markets - you will be scared and emotional about current positions, or annoyed about "possible" positions that you could have opened. These are two factors I hate because it ruins many possible careers of beginner traders.

Hopefully, upon reading this manual you will feel a lot better with the complete idea of forex trading.

-

Best of luck,
Jonas

Jonas Navardauskas
Owner of .4x Team

What is trading?

Trading, simply put, is making a profit off of currency market movements.

However, unlike stocks and company shares - you do not own the currency cross that you are trading; you only have a position in that currency cross.

This means you do not have to worry about buying demand and selling demand of other traders unlike physical shares - where a trader will not want to buy a stock at a high price that you are selling.

The Profit Potential

Due to a trader not owning anything physical - you can earn off of the market losing value AND gaining value.

This alone (in theory) doubles the total profit potential a trader can get over a stock trader or investor.

This could be a problem however as you might be forced out of the position in a loss if the market moves strongly against your open position (this is called getting margined out).

Image 1:APPLE stock price chart, of which you can only make money if the price rises, when you own a part of it.

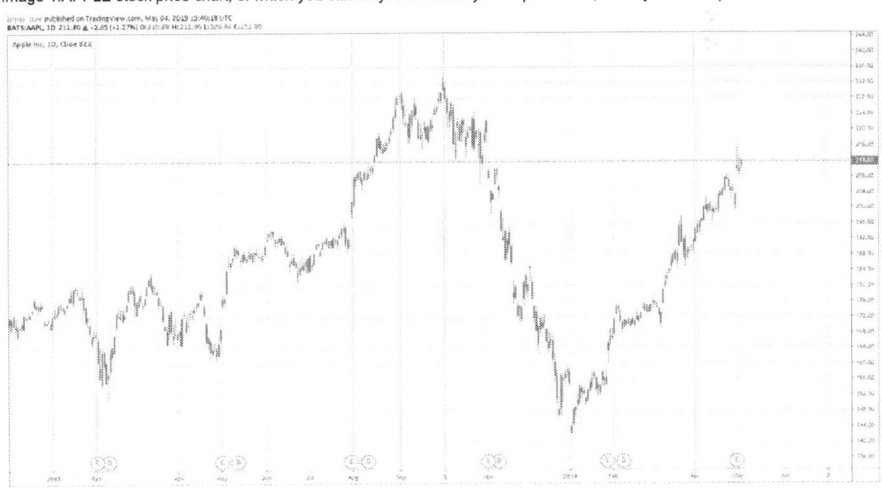

Jonas Navardauskas
Owner of .4x Team

Decision-making

It is all well and good that you can earn money off both market movement directions - however what influences a trader to make a decision in opening a position?

The main distinction between traders is whether they are a "fundamental" trader, or a "technical" trader.

Being a trader based on fundamentals means that news, economic reports and releases are the main method of making trading decisions.

On the other hand, technical traders mostly only work by examining currency cross prices and searching for chart patterns or price action movements on a chart of the currency cross.

The best traders will merge both of these trading styles, due to economic releases causing high volatility in the markets and can speed up the trading process - or some technical traders might avoid trading during times of heavy economic releases as it is often difficult to predict whether the currency will respect previous analysis.

Image 2: Economic Calendar publicly available from https://www.fxstreet.com/economic-calendar, the main source of information for a fundamental trader.

GMT	Time left	Event	Vol.	Actual	Consensus	Previous
MONDAY, MAY 06						
01:45		CNY Caixin Services PMI (Apr)			52.8	54.4
08:00		EUR Markit PMI Composite (Apr)			51.3	51.3
09:00		EUR Retail Sales (YoY) (Mar)			2.3%	2.8%
13:30		USD Fed's Harker speech SPEECH				
17:45		CAD BoC's Governor Poloz speech SPEECH				
22:30		AUD AiG Performance of Construction Index (Apr)				45.6
TUESDAY, MAY 07						
01:30		AUD Retail Sales s.a. (MoM) (Mar)			0.2%	0.8%
01:30		AUD Trade Balance (Mar)			4,250M	4,801M
01:30		AUD Imports (Mar)				-1%
01:30		AUD Exports (Mar)				0%
04:30		AUD RBA Interest Rate Decision (May 7)			1.5%	1.5%
04:30		AUD RBA Rate Statement (May) REPORT				
06:00		EUR Factory Orders s.a. (MoM) (Mar)			0.3%	-4.2%
n/a		NZD GDT Price Index				0.5%
14:00		CAD Ivey Purchasing Managers Index s.a (Apr)			51.1	54.3
14:00		CAD Ivey Purchasing Managers Index (Apr)				57.6
20:00		NZD Monetary Policy Statement REPORT				
23:01		GBP BRC Like-For-Like Retail Sales (YoY) (Apr)				-1.1%
23:50		JPY BoJ Monetary Policy Meeting Minutes REPORT				

Jonas Navardauskas
Owner of .4x Team

Image 3: USD/JPY chart - the main source of information for technical traders.

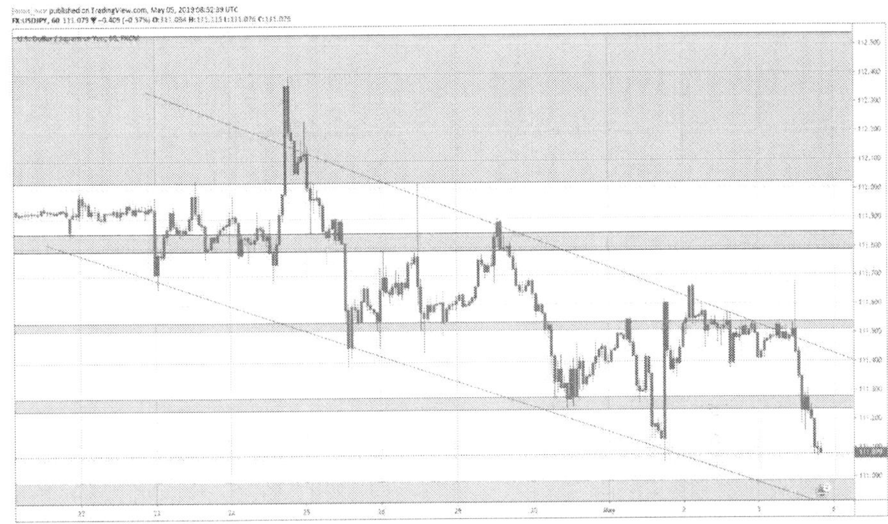

Short-term vs. Long-term trading

The difference between the length of trades is not very important for technical analysis - and there is no fundamentally “better” option and you should instead choose what you prefer as a trader.

It is best to be able to trade both as a “day-trader” (holding positions for less than a day) and a “swing-trader” by holding positions for days, weeks or months. This will allow you to maximise your earning potential, depending on the amount of time you have available to trade.

It is often recommended that people with less time to trade, stick to swing trading, and if you have more time it is probably better to trade as a day-trader as you will learn significantly faster from your own experience due to nearly instantaneous response.

However, due to the foreign exchange market being a 24 hour market it is possible for users with other priorities to trade as a “day-trader” in the evening or night-time.

This manual will document both types of trading and will hopefully assist you in deciding your trading style.

Jonas Navardauskas
Owner of .4x Team

What is technical analysis?

Technical analysis can be difficult for the beginner trader - and is one of the reasons that we teach our students simple, yet effective strategies.

When just starting out, from personal experience, many traders search for the "Holy Grail" system that uses many indicators and instead of working actually causes the learner to grow the completely wrong idea of trading the foreign exchange markets - instead of reading the price data on the chart, the beginner starts analysing the indicator (creating a theory called secondary reasoning) and this will take quite some time to reprogram.

This idealistic view of a "perfect" indicator setup is probably one of the biggest reasons that the majority of forex traders do not remain profitable - as they are often bewildering, wrong and useless in comparison to the raw price data charts.

Technical analysis and crowd psychology

The prices of currency pairs fluctuate due to the trillions of dollars moving in and out of the market at any given moment. Large financial market users such as banks and institutions (also called forex "whales") create the daily market movements that smaller traders attempt to make money off by predicting what they will do.

The main reason why technical analysis continues to work ever since the formation of the modern foreign exchange market in the 1970's is due to all market users following the same or similar emotions during a trade or market movement.

In fact, price action and technical analysis has been around since the 18th century, where the world's most successful price action trader "Munehisa Homma" made the equivalent of $10 billion dollars in the Japanese rice market by only using chart patterns and candlestick price action readings. Therefore, there is no reason to over complicate your trading platform with incessant indicators and instead start trading by taking advantage of other trader's emotions, greed, psyche and general thinking.

When a trader has fully understood this and can start reading the interactions between sellers and buyers only then will they be able to predict any market on any time frame forever.

Technical analysis is often branded as a "self-fulfilling prophecy" due to the majority of the 9.6 million traders in the world all following the same concepts and ideas of technical analysis. Even news outlets and media often refer to moving averages, previous highs/lows and trends - meaning that if you don't over-complicate your own system, you will be following the same trades that millions of others are placing, which causes the market to move in the direction of your trade position.

Image 4: Chart of Tesla's stock price, with clear support and resistance zones where millions of traders make decisions.

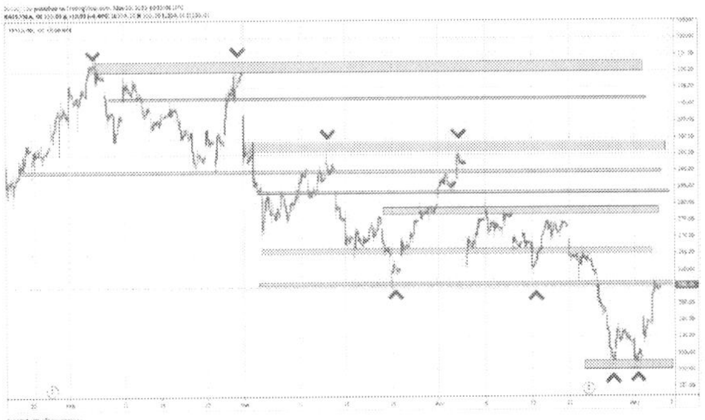

Image 5: Chart of Gold to US Dollar, with clear support and resistance zones where millions of traders make decisions.

Image 6: Chart of Australian Dollar to US Dollar, with clear support and resistance zones where millions of traders make decisions.

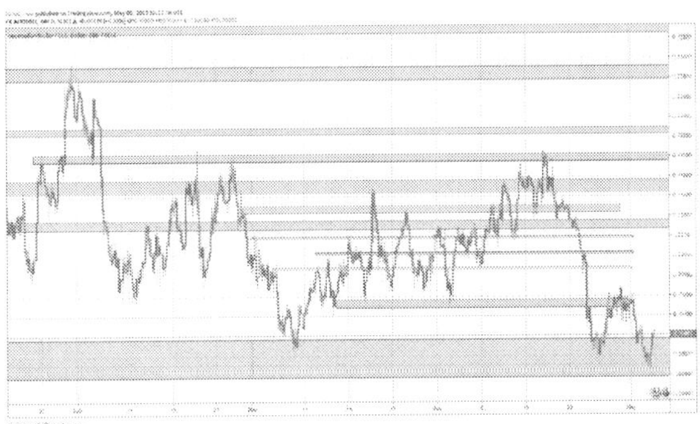

Any market where traders can make instantaneous placements will follow basic technical analysis rules and is easy to take advantage of, as seen in the previous 3 images.

Introduction to candlestick analysis

The first and possibly the most important aspect of technical analysis that this manual will be covering is candlesticks - we will advance through to more complex aspects of trading nearer the end of the manual so that trading is not a foreign topic and you will feel confident about your ability to trade.

Line Charts

Line charts are by far the most easily recognisable form of trading as it is the first view the general population gets when the media talks about share prices, or financial news in papers or magazines.

The line chart fully represents the price maturity of any tradable market or financial value. This is useful as it is easy to analyse directly and see an overshadowing trend as all the information is compressed.

It is clear on a line chart when the market is rising in value or dropping in value. If a market is rising; we often refer to that as a bullish market (as bulls throw victims up) whereas a dropping market is considered a bearish market, as bears "maul" downwards.

On the line chart you only have one piece of data available; the "closing price" which is the price that the session ended on and contains no information within that trading session - maybe the price skyrocketed due to news but was strongly rejected? No information is told about this in a line chart.

Using a line chart is essentially neglecting ¾ of the total information available to a trader.

Image 7: Chart of Great Britain Pound to US Dollar as a line chart - limiting the amount of information usable.

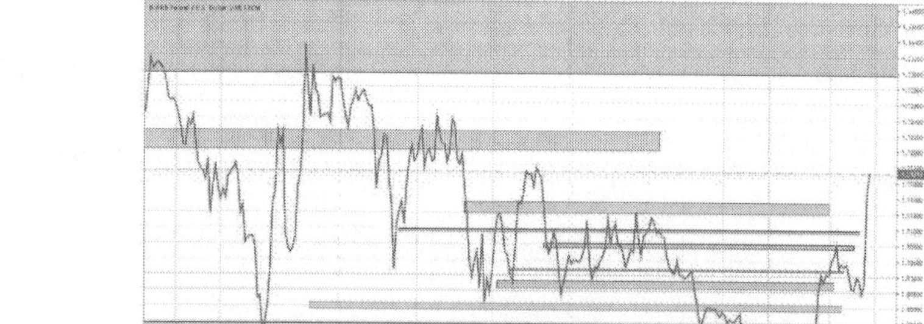

Candlestick Charts

Put simply, candlesticks are a way of communicating information about how price is moving. Candlestick charts are available on the majority of trading platforms for all assets individuals can trade on the platforms.

They do not limit the amount of information displayed at all, unlike line charts and have been in use since the 17th century in Japan.

They are by far the most popular chart type for professional traders.

The Candlestick

Image 8: A monthly US30 Candlestick chart.

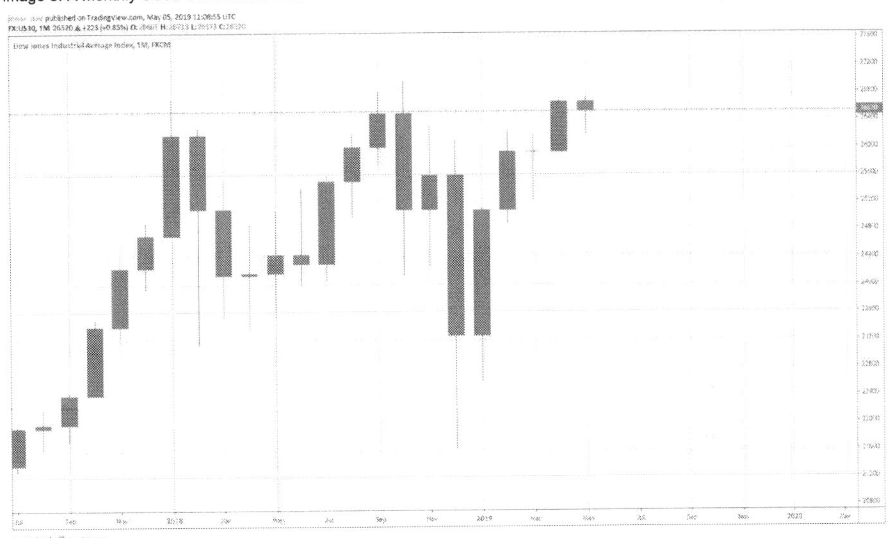

This chart shows price on the right axis, and time on the bottom axis. As well as this, the chart is made of bars that have little lines stemming from the top and the bottom; these are known as wicks.

Overall, the whole thing is considered a "candle".

The candle conveys four pieces of information:
1. The open price
2. The close price
3. The high price
4. The low price

Candles refer to that information for a specific unit of time. For instance, the chart above is a monthly chart; each chart represents one month as the trading session.

Therefore, each candle accounts for the open, close, high, and low price for that given month.

The horizontal axis at the bottom of the chart can be used to understand which month correlates to which candle.

Image 9: Candlestick Infographic

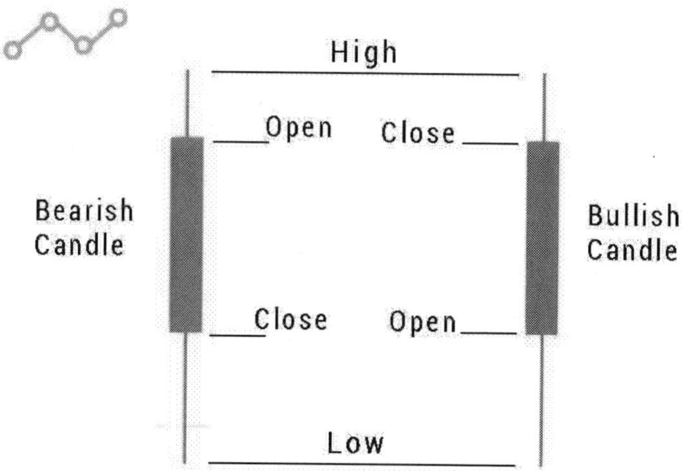

Above is an image that illustrates how those four pieces of information the open, low, high, and close for a given period of time are visualized in the context of a candle:
The wicks, or shadows, are the thin lines that go outside the rectangular body of the candle.

They represent the high and the low price during that time period.

The color of the candle is also significant in understanding whether the open price was higher or lower than the close price.

If the candle is red, or denoted as bearish in some other manner, this means that the open price is lower than the close; and the opposite is true if the candle is green, or denoted as bearish.

In a bearish candle, the price overall closed lower (went down) at the end of the trading session, whereas in a bullish candle, the price overall closed higher (went up) at the end of the trading session.

Image 10: Bearish Candlestick Infographic

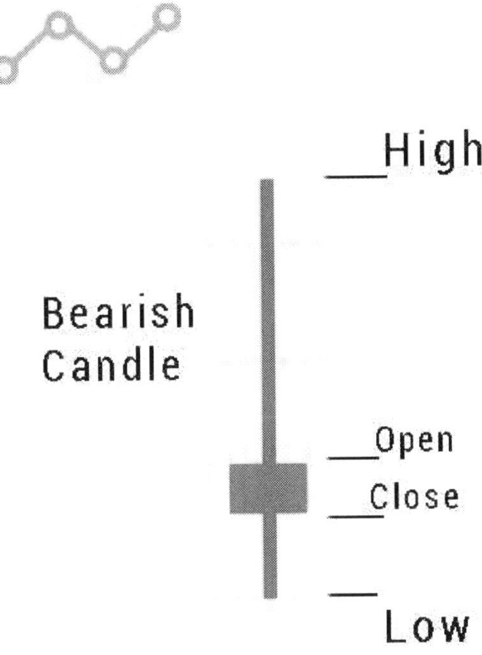

Consider the candle above. The absolute highest point on the candle, the top of the upper line above the rectangular body, is the high price; the absolute lowest point shows how far the price fell during the time period in question.

The top of the candle is the opening price of the time period, while the bottom of the candle is the closing price.

Thus, from this candle, we see that price rallied and fell from its open but bears were ultimately able to push it lower than the open, while bulls came in before the close to push the price up a bit.

Candle Strength Ratio

Let's think about price movements like a war between bulls and bears. Every candlestick is a single battle in an overall war and the 4 elements of the candlestick tell us who is ahead, who is pulling back, who is in control and who has a better chance of winning the next battle.

If one side of the war is stronger, then the financial market will change and fluctuate to represent this.

Bullish market traders predict that the price will move upwards, "buying" the currency cross - moving the total market up and the bearish market traders predict that the price will move downwards, "selling" the currency cross and therefore moving the total market price down.

When one side is stronger the price will either fall or rise accordingly.

In theory, the total market prices act as a market stall with prices determining the supply and demand:

- If the price is relatively low, there will therefore be more bullish traders than bearish traders and this raises the price.
- Once the price raises up very high, the bearish traders find it appropriate to sell and the bullish traders find it too expensive to continue buying.
- The volatility and activity market depend on the disproportion of bearish traders to bullish traders.
- However, when the price is fair for both sellers and buyers, both sides are happy and the market does not fluctuate a lot (this is called consolidation).

This is a key theory as it is the main fundamental analysis for every single currency pair and is all represented in candlesticks.

Candlestick Size

The size of the candlestick is vital in assisting a trader when deciding whether to open a position.

The size of the candlestick, from our previous chapters, represents how much the market has moved in one direction from the open and close in one trading session.

- If a candlestick has an overtly long candlestick body this means that there is more buying or selling interest and represents a strong price fluctuation.
- If in a trend the candlestick body sizes increase, it represents a trend acceleration and indicates that the trend is becoming stronger.
- On the other hand, if the candlestick body sizes decrease, it represents the fact that the trend is slowing down and means the trend is dying down.

Image 11: Clearly decreasing candlestick sizes in a downtrend - indicating a loss of momentum and imminent trend reversal.

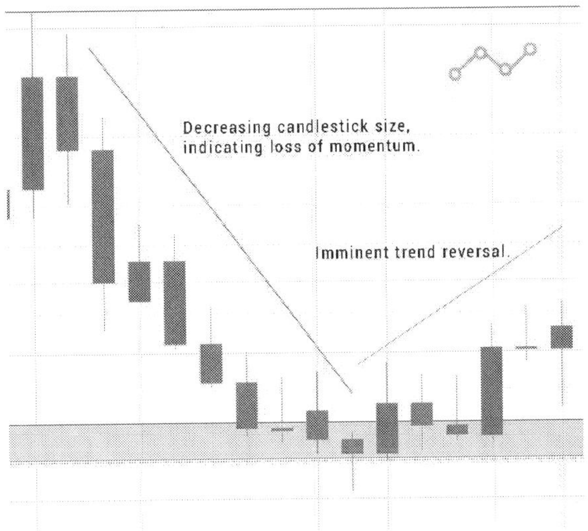

Image 12: Increasing candlestick sizes in a bullish uptrend, followed by a correction and then decreasing bullish candlestick sizes.

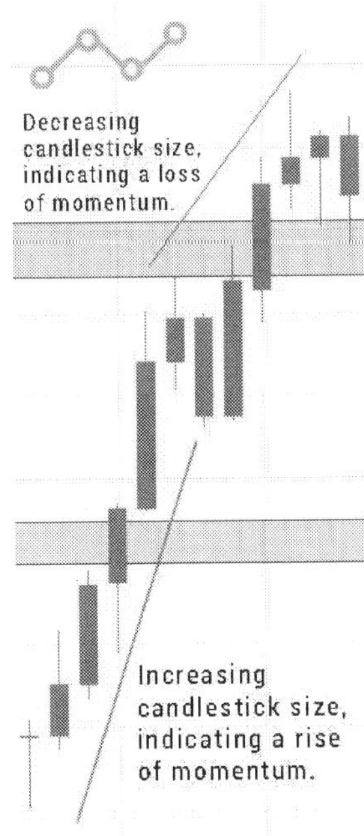

Candle to Wick Ratio

To fully understand market behaviour and crowd psychology, it is important to understand the size of the wick in relation to the size of the candlestick.

- If a trend is consistently strong, with the candle size larger than the wick size means that the trend is maintaining its momentum. This is because you have to imagine the fact that price pushed continually towards the trend direction, and there was no time for any push backwards due to the very strong imbalance of bullish to bearish traders.
- When "trading with the trend" it is important to trade when there is a large candle size, and a small or no candle wick.
- As the trend dies down - the imbalance of bullish to bearish traders starts to shift and wicks start to appear due to the price having been pushed there but rejected.
- Often, a trend stopping is clearly represented by a candle with a small size and a relatively large wick and shows a new balance of the bullish traders to bearish traders meaning they are equal and a strong price movement is imminent.

Image 13: Candlestick wicks appearing on Euro to US Dollar hourly chart.

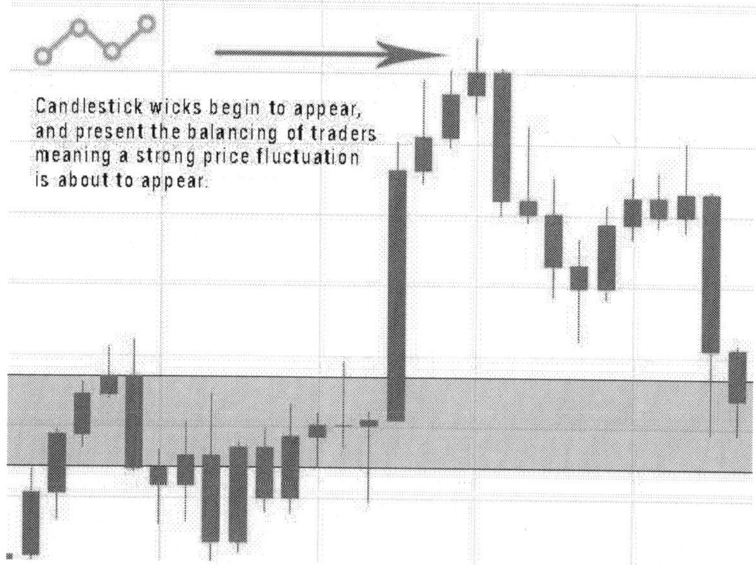

Placement of the wick

Often, if there is a grouping of multiple wicks in a similar price level then this represents a stability and indecision - presenting the possibility for a strong market movement which will by most chance begin the new trend.

However, if all the candles are full with little to no wicks and then a long, sudden wick appears it is by most chance a rejection candlestick - meaning the price has reached a limit where buyers do not want to buy any more and opens up the opportunity for sellers to enter the market and rally the price down. It is the same vice versa.

Mastering the Candlestick Patterns

Doji

This candle has zero or almost zero range between its open and close. Rather than implying potential reversal or the clear dominance of either bears or bulls, these candles suggest indecision or balance between the two forces.

Neither buyers or sellers are fully in control. A doji that occurs in the context of a strong trend implies the weakening of the dominant force that resulted in that trend.

A "long-legged doji" has long wicks in both directions, implying strong, balanced pressure from both buyers and sellers.

Image 14: Doji candle appearing at the top of an uptrend, foreshadowing a balance of buyers and sellers and creating an opportunity for large market movement.

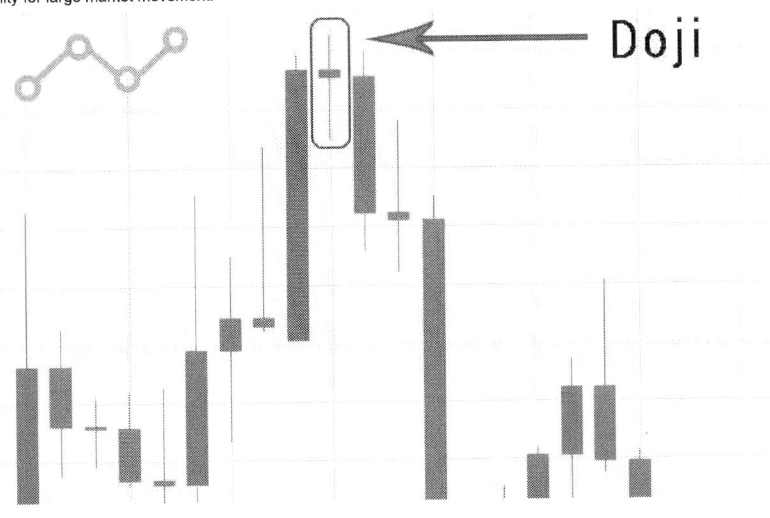

The “dragonfly” and “gravestone” doji imply, respectively, that sellers and buyers controlled the market for most of the trading period, but then the opposite group managed to push the price back to the open before the close

Image 15: Doji, long-legged, dragonfly and gravestone doji candlesticks.

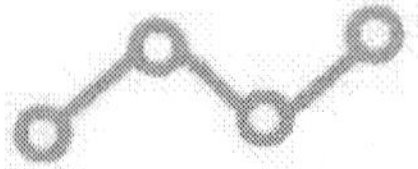

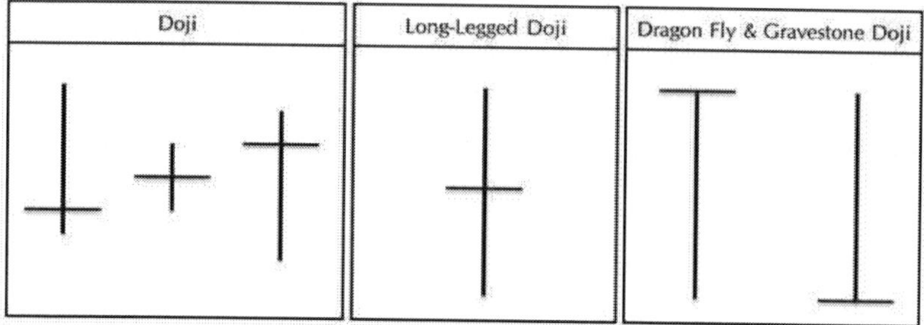

While tradition and long-legged dojis are reflective of indecision and stalling, gravestone and dragonfly are generally clearer, stronger indicators that a force is stepping in to push the market in the direction of the wick and away from the body.

In this respect, gravestone and dragonfly dojis are similar to hammer and hanging man patterns, which are discussed later in this guide.

Hammer

A “hammer” is a candlestick with a small body (a small range from open to close), a long wick protruding below the body, and little to no wick above.

In this respect it is very similar to a dragonfly doji; the primary difference is that a dragonfly doji will have essentially no body, meaning the open and close prices are equal. When a hammer appears at the bottom of a downtrend, its long wick implies an unsuccessful effort by bears to push the price down, and a corresponding effort by bulls to step in and push the price back up quickly before the period closed.

As such, a hammer candlestick in the context of a downtrend suggests the potential exhaustion of the downtrend and the onset of a bullish reversal.

The “neckline,” often determined by the high of the previous bar, is the level that price must hit on the next candlestick in order to confirm the hammer’s reversal signal.

Image 16: Hammer candle appearing on the daily USD/JPY chart showing clear rejection.

Hanging Man

The "hanging man" is the name given to a candle that is identical in shape to the hammer; the difference is that while hammers occur in downtrends, the hanging man pattern occurs in uptrends.

In this case, the wick extends down, contrary to the uptrend, and suggests the emergence of bearish demand capable of pushing the price down. It is often the first sign that the uptrend is exhausting, and bears are stepping in to create a reversal.

For the reversal signal to be confirmed, the consequent bearish bar should reach the "neckline" established by the open of the bullish bar on the other side of the hanging man.

Image 17: Hanging man candle appearing on the 4 hour AUD/USD chart.

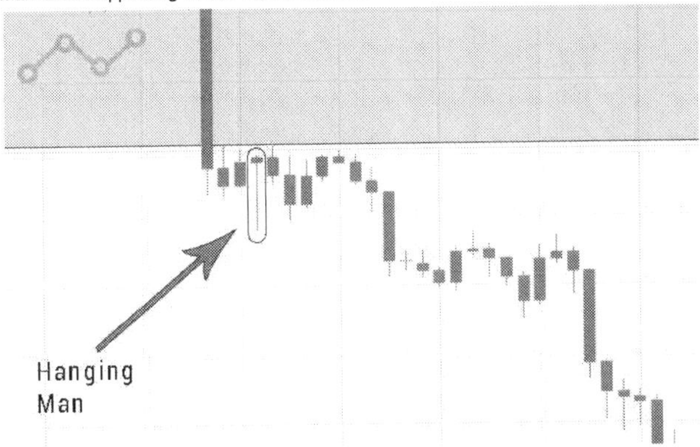

Shooting Star

This candlestick is simply the inversion of the hanging man: it has a small body and a long wick protruding above it, with little to no wick below.

The "shooting star" occurs at the height of an uptrend; its long wick implies that resistance to further bullish movement has been encountered above the close, and a bearish reversal may be imminent. In this case, a strong red candle or a price at the level of the previous bar's open can act as confirmation or an entry point.

Often, shooting stars are further characterized by a gap between the previous bars close and the relatively higher open of the shooting star.

Image 18: Shooting star candle appearing on the weekly CAD/CHF chart.

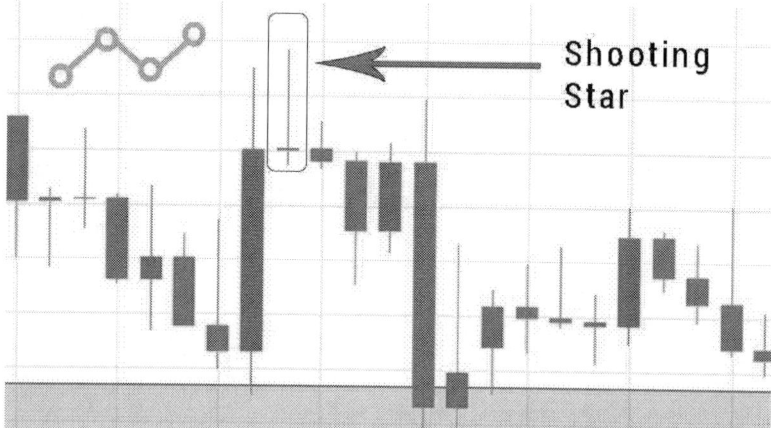

Checkmate

Checkmates occur when price becomes locked in a narrow trading range preceding a reversal in direction.

In a typical bearish checkmate (below), an uptrend meets a resistance level that is tested and then rejected due to consequent pressure from holding the level. In these cases, the checkmate begins as the first candle in the range reaches a high that the pressure from bulls is unable to surpass.

Price remains deadlocked in a tight trading range before the range is broken with a long bearish candlestick, indicating that the reversal has begun.

Image 19: Resistance Level Checkmate on the EUR/USD hourly chart.

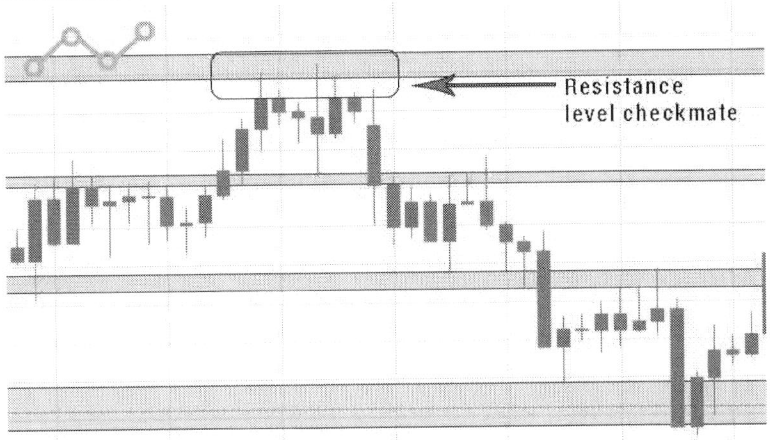

As an entry signal, this pattern requires confirmation from one or two strong bearish bars.

In a bullish checkmate (below), the opposite occurs, typically at a support rather than resistance level.

Image 20: Support level checkmate on the EUR/USD hourly chart.

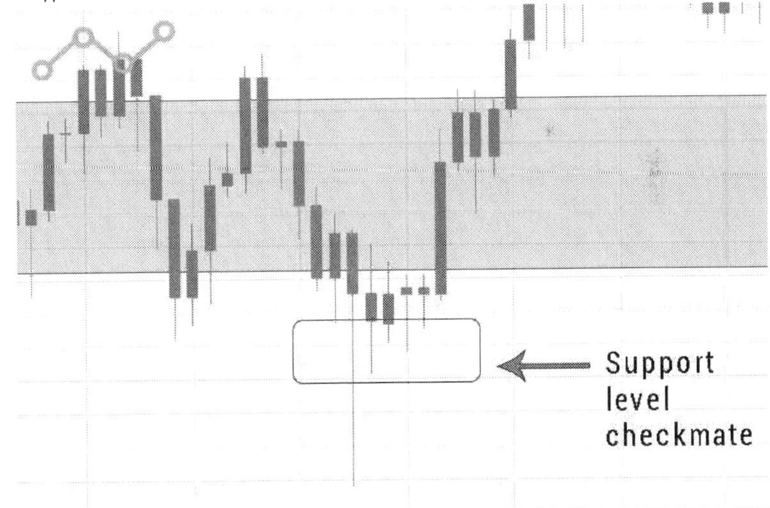

The long lower wick of the first pinbar in the box establishes a low that the bears cannot achieve; price is trapped thereafter in a narrow trading range, the checkmate, until bulls successfully reverse the trend.

The tall green bar immediately after the box confirms the bullish reversal. In the patterns that have been presented thus far, a simple concept should be emerging: when a long wick appears in the context of a trend, it often signals a potential reversal of that trend.

Evening Star

The "evening star" is the small-bodied middle candle of a 3-bar pattern that can provide an early indication of a reversal from a bullish to a bearish trend, typically with an opening price at or a gap above the close of the previous candle (a gap indicates space between the body of the previous candle and the open of the consequent candle).

The pattern represents a potential top, and therefore a potential signal to sell.

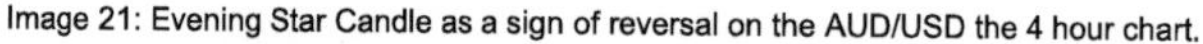

Image 21: Evening Star Candle as a sign of reversal on the AUD/USD the 4 hour chart.

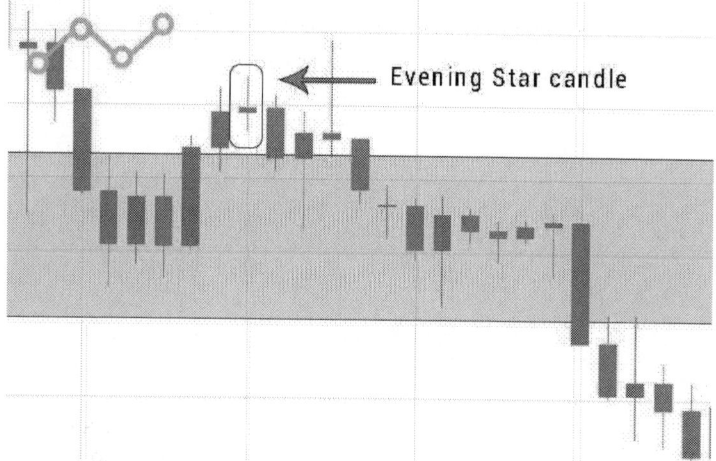

These are the characteristics of the three candles:

- A long bullish candle
- A small-bodied bullish or bearish candle or a doji that opens at or above the close of the previous candle.
- A red candle that opens at or below the low point of the previous candle's body and closes at or below the center of the first candle.

In order for the pattern to be valid, the sequence of candles must be as described above. Moreover, the pattern should appear in the context of an uptrend in order to signal a reversal and the start of a downtrend.

Morning Star

The "morning star" is the inverse of the evening star, a 3-bar pattern in which the "star" is a small-bodied candle, typically opening at the close of the previous candle or opening a gap below it, indicating that a trend is transitioning from bearish to bullish.

Image 22: Morning Star Candle as a sign of reversal on the AUD/JPY daily chart.

The morning star constitutes a potential bottom to the preceding bearish leg, and functions therefore as a buy signal.

A green bullish candle that opens at or above the high point of the previous candle and closes at or above the center of the first candle.

While an evening star pattern after an uptrend signals a reversal, the opposite of a morning star pattern in a downtrend can also signal reversal, and a change in the balance of power between bears and bulls.

Bullish Engulfing

In this pattern, the real body of a bearish candle (the range from open to close) is encompassed by the body of a consequent bullish candle. This indicates an increase in activity from both bears and bulls, and a shift of overall market sentiment towards bullishness.

Like with all the patterns we've discussed thus far, this pattern should be viewed in consideration of the trend at the time: if a bullish engulfing pattern appears in a downtrend, it can suggest a shift price trend and the onset of buying demand becoming the prevailing force that will ultimately push the price higher in the context of the timeframe being viewed.

Image 23: Bullish Engulfing candle on the daily CAD/CHF chart.

Bearish Engulfing

This pattern is the converse of a bullish engulfing pattern, wherein the body of a bullish candle is encompassed by the body of a consequent bullish candle.

This indicates an increase in activity from both bears and bulls, and a shift of market sentiment towards bearishness. As we have observed with other patterns, the context of the trend is critical; a bearish engulfing pattern is most indicative of the onset of a bearish price move when it appears in the midst of an uptrend.

Image 24: Bearish Engulfing candle on the hourly CAD/CHF chart.

Harami/Inside Bar

This pattern is a two-candlestick pattern in which the first candlestick vertically encompasses the one that follows it.

This signal is interpreted in two ways:

- An indication that an increase in volatility is imminent. This affords traders the opportunity to create trades that speculate not so much on direction, but rather on an increase in volatility on a breakout in any specific direction.
- In the context of a trend, a harami/inside bar can be indicative of exhaustion and the onset of a reversal. In this manner, it is similar to the "long wick" patterns and evening star/morning star patterns examined earlier in this guide.

Image 25: Bullish Inside Bar on the daily NZD/USD chart.

Piercing Line

A bullish signal that occurs in the context of a downtrend when, after a long bearish candle, a bullish candle opens at a new low and then closes at a level at least halfway up the body of the previous bar; this signal is reliable as a two-bar indicator of a trend reversal in proportion to the height of the second bullish bar.

Image 26: Piercing Line set-up present on the GBP/USD weekly chart.

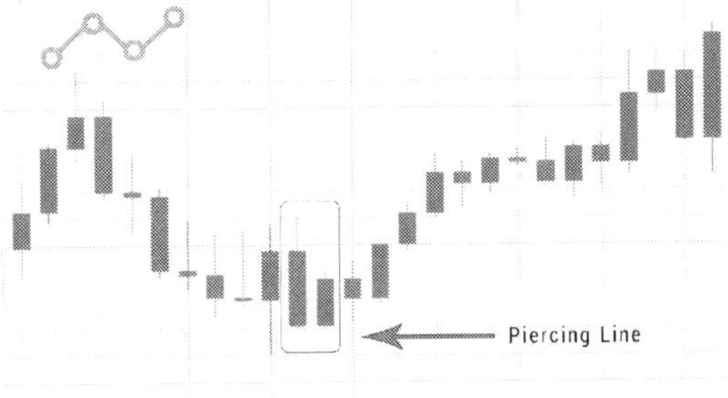

Dark Cloud Cover

This two-candle bearish reversal pattern is the bearish converse of the piercing line, occurring at the top of a bullish trend.

The first bullish candle is followed by a bearish candle that opens at a new high and then closes at least halfway down the body of the bar preceding it.

The strength of the reversal signal is proportionate to the length of the second candle.

Image 27: Dark Cloud Cover on the monthly GBP/AUD chart.

This pattern is clearly conceptually and mathematically similar to the Piercing Line.

Three White Soldiers

This is a 3-candle bullish pattern that implies a reversal at the bottom of a bearish trend. The three soldiers are bullish candlesticks that open within the body of the previous candlestick and close near the high of the day.

This applies to all three candles; they should all be strong bullish candles, with small wicks and a close near the top.

These high closes imply a strong reversal from bearish to bullish market sentiment.

Image 28: Three White Soldiers candle setup present on the GBP/JPY daily chart.

Three Black Crows

This 3-candle pattern is the opposite of "Three White Soldiers;" it signals the reversal away from bullish control at the top of an uptrend.

It consists of three successive bearish bars that open within the preceding bar's body and close below its close.

Image 29: Three Black Crows candle setup present on the GBP/JPY hourly chart.

Chart Composition

The step after understanding candlestick movements and candlestick patterns, it is to learn the different, vitally important, chart patterns.

In my opinion, chart compositions and patterns are more important than individual candle analysis due to chart patterns including many candlesticks and containing significantly more information.

In my personal trading style I will base trades off of chart compositions but will ignore a potential trade if the candlesticks do not support the trade idea - or use a tighter stop loss in this situation.

Market Cycles

During price movement in a chart - it is always in one of three stages: either the overall price of the currency cross is rising, falling or staying still and moving sideways in a range.

The main classifications professional traders make in a moving chart are:

Range Trading

- Without a clear trend in the forex market, the market tends to maintain movement in a "box"-like range. The price fluctuates between typical "support" and "resistance" lines and is very simple to predict.
- The bullish traders attempt to lift the price, but they are met at a certain resistance zone, where the bearish traders believe it is expensive enough to sell.

Image 30: Consolidation/Box range on the 4 hour XAU/USD chart.

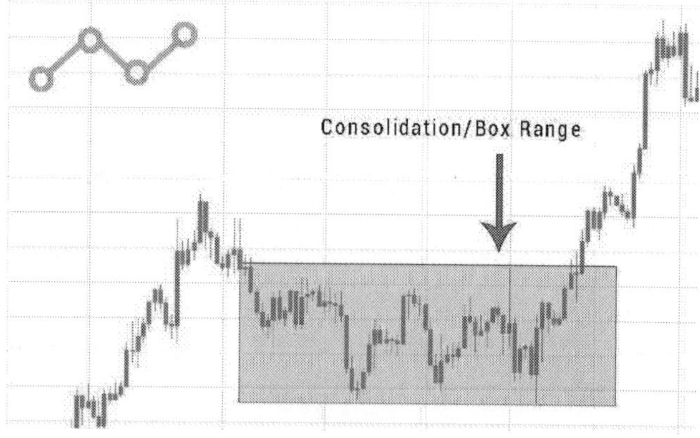

- If the price moves below the previously analysed "range" it is by most chance that the price will return to the "box" and continue the range trading.
- These range movements will always finish in a breakout, which is the second main classification traders make.
- The longer the range movements happen, the bigger the breakout and often causes a "rally" (a strong, longer upwards market movement).

Market Breakouts

- This is the feature of the chart cycle where it stops continually trending inside of a box range and "breaks-out" of the previous pre-decided market movements and begins trading in positive or negative trends.
- The breakout cycle can vary in strength and technique. It is difficult to predict what style of breakout it will be without witnessing the beginning of the trend.

The first and often most popular breakout technique is where the market price moves either directly down or directly up and acts very volatile in a short period of time.

- If a trader wants to make profit off this breakout method, it is recommended to only enter at the start of the breakout or to not enter the position at all. This is because if you enter a trade late it might result in consolidation or a retracement.

Image 31: Consolidation/Box range on the 4 hour XAU/USD chart followed by an uncontrolled, volatile breakout resulting in ~300 pips in less than 20 hours.

The other breakout method is more sustainable and it is where the price breaks out and continually staggers, but soon breakouts out in the same original direction.

- The market in this breakout technique is not so volatile, and is usually just a technical breakout instead of a fundamental news change.
- When this happens, it is often that the price will keep stalling and consolidating as it continues in one direction.
- Every swing, the market will reach a new high or low.
- An important factor about these breakouts is that the moving average begins to increase and can cause a new consolidation that becomes the previous "trading-range" cycle.

Image 32: Consolidation/Box range on the 4 hour XAU/USD chart followed by a stable, controlled breakout.

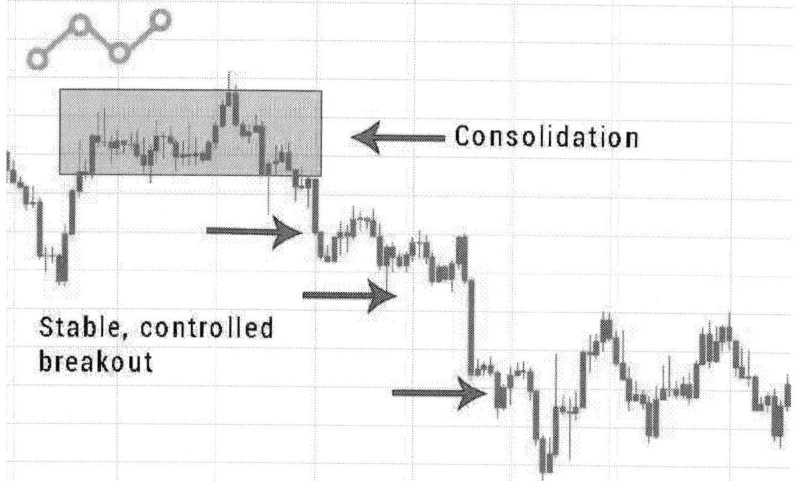

Market Rest

- Once a rally or sell-off has occurred in the market, it is unsure what will happen next in the market. The market cycle must restart.
- In this situation, it is very difficult to predict what will happen next in the market even with the use of indicators - and is therefore strongly recommended to ignore the market in these conditions and move on to a different currency crossover.

Price Swings

During a breakout period from a previous consolidation, the market acts volatile in one direction.

When a trader realises the breakout period and enters the position in the direction of the trend, the trader will set out their risk:reward ratio, and then close their position when they are happy with their pip count for the trade.

The trader must then close out their position and in theory open a new counter-position - this will then cause a mini-correction against the trend - this becomes a swing low for the trend. When the trend then later continues in the original direction it will form a new swing high.

Image 33: Price Swings displayed on the 4 hour Great Britain Pound to Japanese Yen chart.

As long as there are consistent higher swing highs, and higher swing lows - this means the market is in an uptrend and vice-versa for downtrends - this is why it is often recommended for beginner traders to only "trade with the trend" as it will usually result in more successful trades.

This simple idea of swing highs and lows determines the key technical change of a trend reversal - which is what many high risk/reward trades begin with.

Market Swing Duration

When a market swing happens, the intensity and most importantly the duration of a one-sided market rally is what determines whether bulls or bears are in control of the market.

For example; a strong, long rally to the upside which does not have any long corrections or retracements and features long candlesticks with small wicks - presents the fact that the bulls have control of the market.

Image 34: Differentiation in market swing duration on the Canadian Dollar to Japanese Yen Hourly chart.

However, market movement in the opposite side in a sell-off shows traders that the bears currently have most of the market.

The opposite of this entire idea can be used when the market movement is staggered and delayed - and this shows that the market movement is weak and even though the market is moving in one direction constantly neither the bulls or the bears have a very strong market control.

Market Swing Acceleration

The acceleration/rate at which a market swings is also vital - it tells us as traders whether a market trend is sustainable and the probability of a key reversal.

When the steepness of a market movement is very high it creates the opportunity for a "V" market formation where the price reverses in the opposite direction with the same steepness and acceleration of the previous trend.

This is a great opportunity to catch a fast amount of pips - you enter the trade when the market has already started reversing with a very tight stop loss as if there will be a large amount of drawdown, then the market has not started reversing fully yet and instead you should wait for another scenario.

Image 35: The Great British Pound to Australian Dollar presenting a strong upwards swing acceleration, followed by a crash.

Therefore, when the market change is very steep - it is not recommended to partake in the original direction of the breakout - but instead wait for the reversal.

Market Swing Confluence

The previous ideas of market swing durations, and market swing acceleration can be joined together to create more probable and stronger signals where you can place larger lot sizes to make a larger percentage profit from the same equity.

For example, if the market swing has a long duration with a weak acceleration at the start - but then increases in trend line acceleration this means the overall trend strength is increasing and creates a stronger signal to follow the trend.

Market Structure

As a trader, I often refer to market structure or market tendencies to be either "upward" or "downward" - which comes from many aspects including key support/resistance levels, market swing duration/acceleration, price action confluence e.t.c

The main aspect of market structure is how easily the market breaks new highs or new lows. If the market struggles and consolidated excessively a new level - I will be more wary of entering new breakouts as it might be time for a market reversal.

If the market completely reverses after making a new market high - this represents market fatigue/exhaustion and clearly represents that this market phase is over and it might reverse just as quickly as it reached this level (called a "V" market formation).

Image 36: The Daily US30 chart portraying a generally upwards structure, due to higher highs and market swing analysis.

This idea is often used by professional traders - where if you trade a breakout, and the market begins to consolidate, the trader will enter new positions upon consolidation and place the stop losses for all positions right above or below the highest/lowest levels of the consolidation zone.

This is because when the market breaks through this consolidation zone in the wrong direction - the whole market structure is scrapped and new trade ideas must be found. This ensures that you are not stuck in a trade where you are “hoping” and instead are doing what the market shows you, not what you think it is doing.

The Most Vital Chart Patterns

Chart patterns are specific price formations on a chart that predict future price movements. As technical analysis is based on the assumption that history repeats itself, popular chart patterns have shown that a specific price movement is following a particular formation of price (chart pattern) with high probability.

Therefore, chart patterns are grouped into (1) continuation patterns – that signal a continuation of the underlying trend, and (2) reversal patterns – that signal reversal of the underlying trend.

Mastering the Chart Patterns

Head and Shoulders

Head and Shoulders is a reversal chart pattern, that indicates the underlying trend is about to change. It consists of three swing highs, with the middle swing high being the highest.

After the middle swing high, a lower high occurs which signals that buyers didn't have enough strength to pull the price higher. The pattern looks like a head with a left and right shoulder (the three swing highs), and that's how it got its name.

The neckline is connecting the two shoulders, and a break-out below the neckline is considered a selling signal.

If the Head and Shoulders pattern occurs during a downtrend, the same inverse pattern (with three swing lows) is called an Inverse Head and Shoulders pattern.

Image 37: Head and Shoulders formation on the weekly GBP/JPY chart.

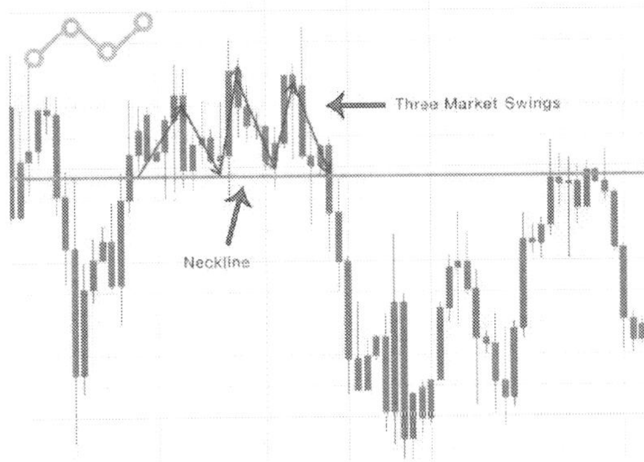

Double Top and Double Bottom

Double Top and Double Bottom are another reversal pattern, occurring during up- and downwards trend, respectively. A double top, as the name suggests, has two swing highs at about the same, or slightly different prices.

The example below shows that buyers didn't manage to push the price higher, and a trend reversal might be ahead. The trigger signal for opening a sell position is the break of the support line, and a double bottom pattern is the opposite, with two swing lows.

Image 38: Double Top Formation on the weekly GBP/JPY chart.

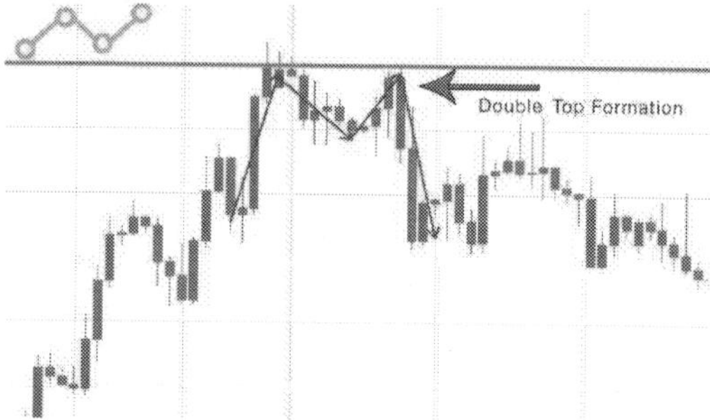

Triple Top and Triple Bottom

Triple Top and Triple Bottom formations are basically the same as Double Top and Double Bottom formations. Both are reversal patterns, with the difference that Triple Tops and Bottoms have three swing highs and swing lows, respectively.

Image 39: Triple Top Formation on the 4 hour GBP/JPY chart.

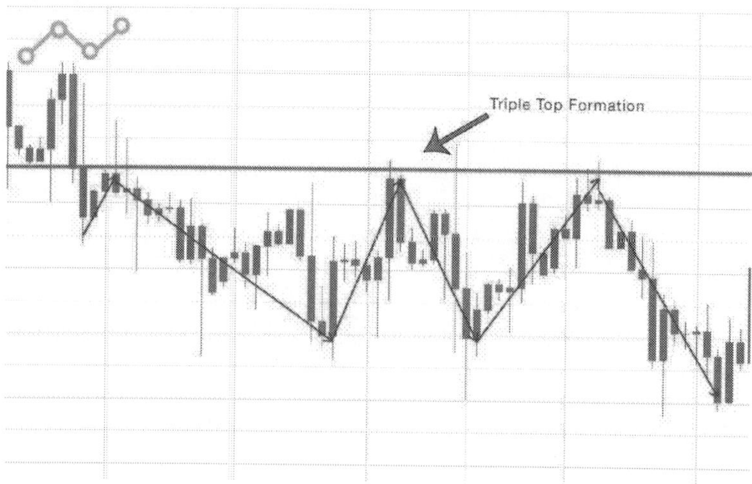

Trigger signals are again the break of support and resistance lines, with target prices being the distance between the top and support line (for Triple Tops), and bottom and resistance line (for Triple Bottoms).

Rounding Top

A Rounding Top pattern takes a little longer to form than the other mentioned chart patterns. It shows a gradual change of the sentiment from bullish to bearish.

The price forms gradually a „rounded top", as can be seen on the chart. The trigger for entering a short position is the break of the support line, with the price target equal the distance from the top to the support line.

Image 40: Rounding Top Formation on the daily GBP/JPY chart.

Rounding Bottom

A Rounding Bottom is a Rounding Top flipped vertically. The price made a gradual change from the previous downtrend, indicated by a „rounded bottom".

The trigger signals are the same as by the Rounding Top, i.e. the break of the resistance line. Price target is the distance between the bottom and the resistance line.

Image 41: Rounding Bottom Formation

Rectangle

A rectangle is a continuation pattern, which means it confirms that the underlying trend should continue. It is divided into bullish and bearish rectangles, depending on the underlying trend. A bullish rectangle appears during an uptrend when the price enters a consolidation phase, during a sideways trading.

The price will likely break out in the direction of the preceding trend. The trigger signal is the break of the upper line of the rectangle, with the price target being the height of the rectangle.

Image 42: Downward continuation rectangle formation on the hourly GBP/JPY chart.

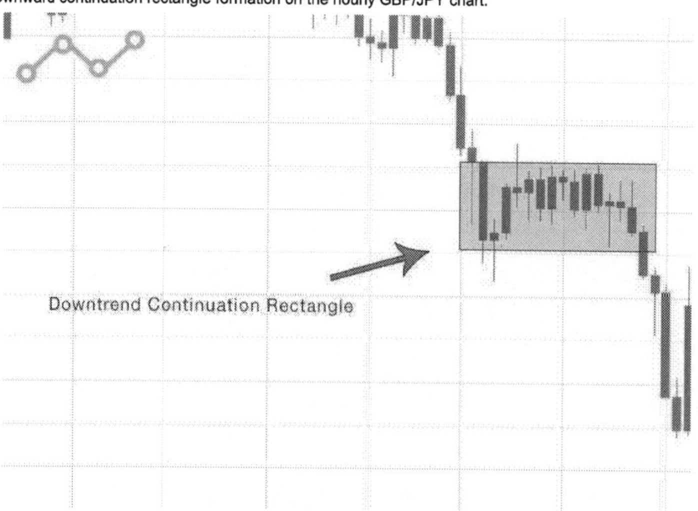

For the bearish rectangle, the opposite rules apply. It forms during a prevailing downtrend, when the price enters a congestion phase and trades sideways. This means the trend will most likely continue downwards, with the break of the lower rectangle line. The price target is again the height of the rectangle.

Wedges

A wedge is another continuation pattern. A bullish wedge forms during an uptrend, as the price trades inside converging trendlines. These converging trend-lines imply that sellers are trying to push the price lower, but don't have enough strength to win against the buyers.

Ultimately, the buyers win and the price breaks through the upper trendline, indicating that the uptrend will resume.

A bearish wedge is similar to a bullish one, with the difference that it is appearing during downtrends, and the slope of the wedge is up. Converging trend-lines are again showing that buyers interrupted the downtrend, trying to push prices higher.

A break-out through the lower trendline indicates that sellers won the battle, and the downtrend is resuming. The target price is, like by bullish wedges, the maximal height of the wedge which is then projected to the point of break-out.

Image 43: Rising Wedge formation on the hourly EUR/NZD chart.

Flags

A flag is very similar to a wedge, with the difference that the trendlines which form the flag are parallel, and not converging. A flag pole is also a part of the flag pattern, because the target price is measured in a different way than by other chart patterns. Flags can be bullish and bearish, with a bullish flag shown on the chart above.

A bullish flag forms during an uptrend, with parallel trend-lines above and below the price-action, which form a down slope. A break-out above confirms that the uptrend is resuming. A bearish flag is pretty much the same as a bullish flag, with the difference that it forms during downtrends and has an up slope.

The price target is measured as the height of the flagpole (the arrow) to the top of the flag, which is then projected to the lowest point of a bullish flag (or highest point of a bearish flag).

Image 44: Flag formation seen on the weekly AUD/JPY chart.

Triangles

Triangles can be ascending, descending and symmetrical. All three types of triangles look pretty much the same, with the difference that ascending triangles have a flat upper trendline, and descending triangles a flat lower trendline.

A symmetrical trendline is the most common, and forms during both up- and downtrends. It has converging trendlines, just like a wedge pattern, but the slope is neither pointing up or down.

The breakout point of the lower trendline during downtrends confirms that the downtrend is resuming, while a breakout of the upper trendline during uptrends confirm the underlying uptrend. The target price is the height of the triangle, projected to the point of the breakout.

Image 45: Symmetrical Triangle Formation on 4 hour XAU/USD (Spot Gold) chart.

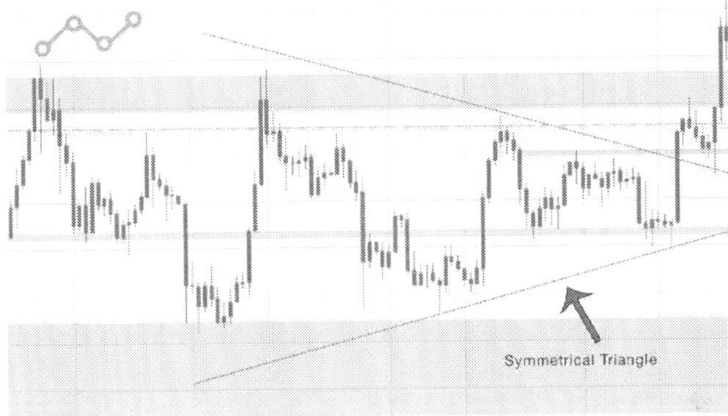

Cup and Handle

A Cup and Handle pattern is a Rounding Top pattern with an additional pullback (the handle).

It is a continuation pattern which shows that in the middle of an uptrend, the sellers tried to push the price lower, but the sentiment is again gradually changing from the sellers to the buyers.

Additionally, a pullback occurs as the last attempt of the sellers to dominate. After a break-out of the resistance line (the bold line), the target price is calculated as the height of the Cup & Handle pattern.

Image 46: Cup and Handle formation seen on the US30 (Dow Jones Index) daily chart.

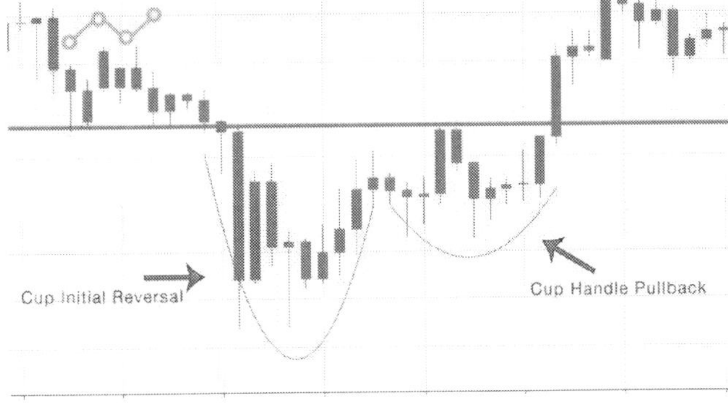

ras

n

& Handle pattern appears during downtrends, and the inverse rules of a
landle apply for it.

Indicators

The Use of Indicators

Misrepresenting Price

To put plainly, indicators are another method of representing the current price level - all indicators use the same information found in a normal candlestick chart.

For example, indicators such as moving averages use a certain number of previous candle closing prices and represents this in a line on the chart and can present the overall trend of the market to you instantly; however, the same can be achieved by understanding the information represented in a japanese candlestick chart as you have all the data that indicators reform to represent in a line form - but could influence your trading decisions negatively due to overcomplication.

Generally, I do not recommend the use of indicators due the overcomplication on the chart - and refrains you from developing as a trader and learning to read the raw price presented. As well as this, some indicators cannot properly represent the most vital aspects of the chart, such as support and resistance levels.

Image 47: The RSI indicator, and the key zones and levels it represents.

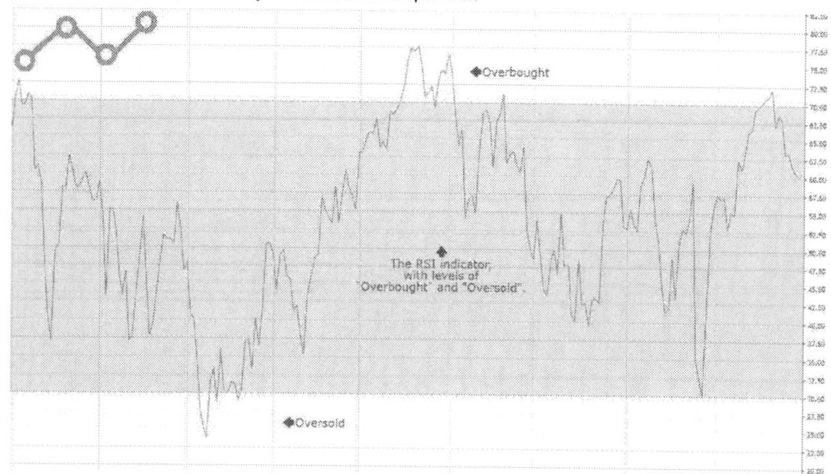

For example, a highly popular indicator among both successful and unsuccessful traders is the Relative Strength Index (R.S.I). The use of R.S.I originally appeared in individual stock charting e.g. Apple and Microsoft.

The R.S.I is a momentum indicator, and if used properly should in theory represent when an asset is “overbought” or “oversold” and if there is potential for a reversal - this is useful in a trending market, when you have clear supply and demand zones with little to no corrections and the R.S.I “swings” smoothly from overbought to oversold following the market movement.

On the other hand, a currency cross or pair cannot be “oversold” or “overbought” as the cross only represent a ratio of one currency price to another.

Indicator Classification

There are many indicators available to retail traders, and so they have to be classified into categories due to some indicators being very similar to one another - and provide similar information because they are based on calculations that do not differ from one another very much.

These indicators can be classified into three categories.

- ### Trending Indicators

Trending indicators, as their name suggests, identify and follow the trend of a currency pair. Forex traders make most of their money when currency pairs are trending.

It is therefore crucial for you to be able to determine when a currency pair is trending and when it is consolidating.

Image 48: The most popular trending indicator, the moving average, on the hourly Australian Dollar to Swiss Franc chart.

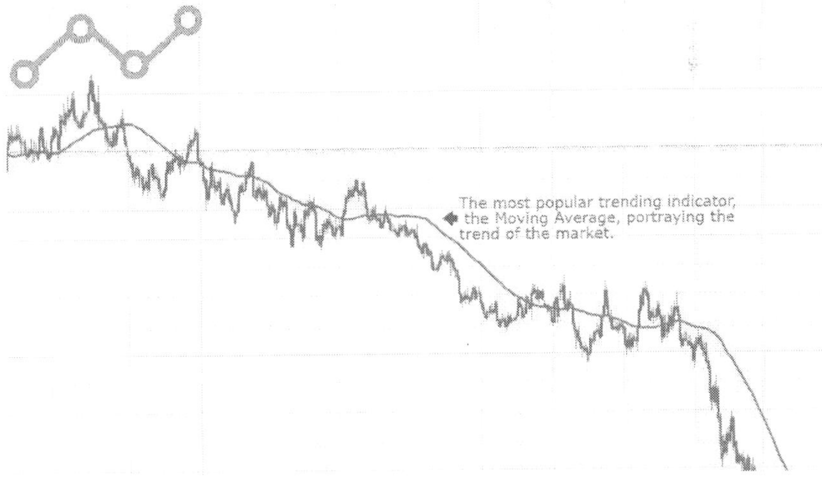

If you can enter your trades shortly after a trend begins and exit shortly after the trend ends, you will be quite successful.

- ## Oscillating Indicators

Oscillating indicators, as their name suggests, are indicators that move back and forth as currency pairs rise and fall.

Oscillating indicators can help you determine how strong the current trend of a currency pair is and when that trend is in danger of losing momentum and turning around.

When an oscillating indicator moves too high, the currency pair is considered to be overbought (too many people have bought the currency pair and there are not enough buyers left in the market to push the currency pair higher). This indicates the currency pair is at risk of losing momentum and turning around to move lower or sideways.

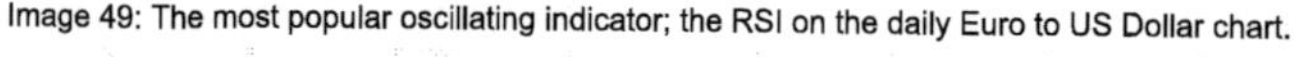

Image 49: The most popular oscillating indicator; the RSI on the daily Euro to US Dollar chart.

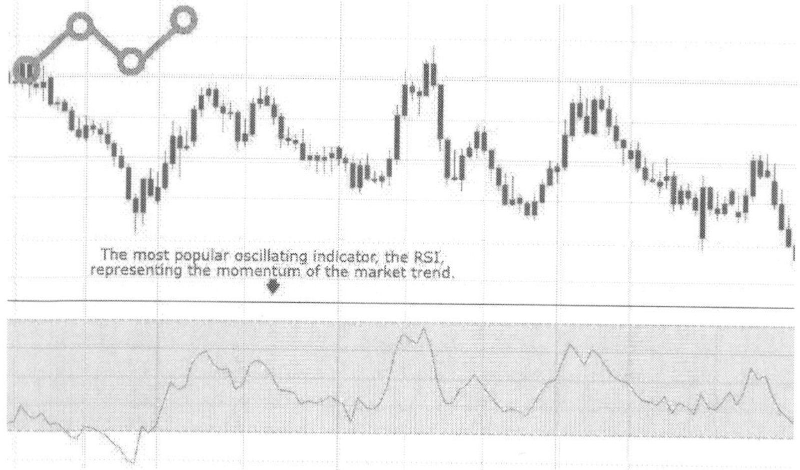

When an oscillating indicator moves too low, the currency pair is considered to be oversold (too many people have sold the currency pair and there are not enough sellers left in the market to push the currency pair lower).

This indicates the currency pair is at risk of losing momentum and turning around to move higher or sideways.

- ## Volume/Volatility Indicators

Since currencies are traded on the inter-bank market and not on a central exchange, volume data for currency transactions is not available.

Image 50: The volume indicator represented on the US Dollar to Candian Dollar hourly chart.

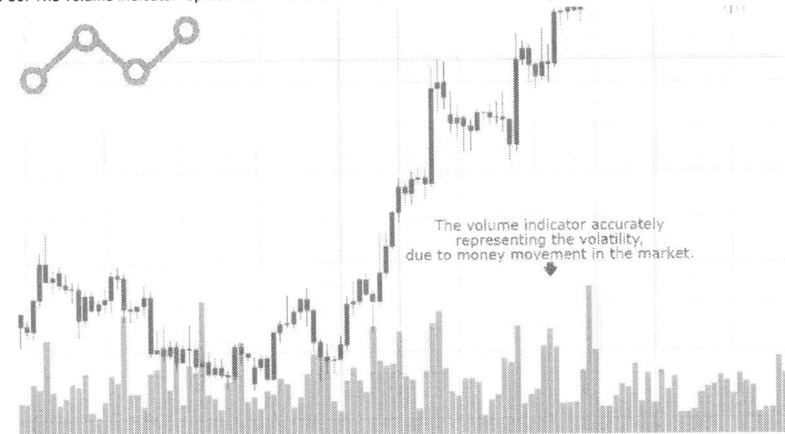

Without volume data, you cannot construct volume indicators. Therefore, we do not use volume indicators in Forex trading - however, we do recommend learning about them and their forex counterparts; the volatility indicators.

The volatility indicators decide how volatile the current market movement is - knowing this can be useful to know when to enter or avoid entering and decide take profit distances and stop losses.

Number of Indicators

When deciding how many indicators you should use, it is incredibly important to understand that using more than one indicator from each group is unintelligent - due to each of the indicators in the same group providing the same signals and ideas.

Image 51: Three oscillating indicators on the daily gold (XAU/USD) chart all providing similar information.

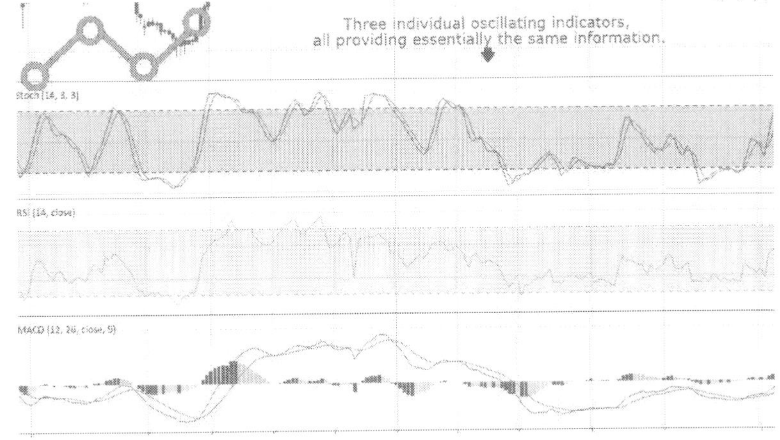

This may be damaging to your trades, as a trader might assume that if both indicators are suggesting a similar movement - they will value it as a separate confluence factor, where it shouldn't as it is based on the same calculations.

Moving Averages

Moving averages are the most basic trending indicator. They show you what direction a currency pair is going and where potential levels of support and resistance may be — moving averages themselves can serve as both support and resistance and are referred to as dynamic levels of support and resistance - and act like exact levels instead of zones.

They are also the most popular indicators across all financial instruments and are featured in television, news and financial papers - therefore they are often respected quite clearly on larger timeframes.

Image 52: Visible respect and rejection on the 4 hour Australian Dollar to Japanese Yen from the 21 period Moving Average.

Construction of Moving Averages

Moving averages are constructed by finding the average closing price of a currency pair at any given time and then plotting these points on a price chart as a continuous line.

The result gives you a smooth line that follows the price movement of the currency pair. You can adjust the volatility and speed of a moving average by adjusting the number of candles the indicator takes into account.

Moving Average Signals

Filtering out Trades

A moving average can be used to abruptly cut out 50% of all trades, and will often improve your general trade accuracy and results.

By only considering trades in the direction of the moving average indicator, you can differentiate between more risky trades and higher probability trades.

This means that you should only enter a long position if the price is in an overall uptrend and vice versa. This is because if you get a bad entry into your trade, but the overall trend continues - the market is more forgiving and you will not face much drawdown, or be in drawdown for very long.

The opposite can be said for trading against the overall trend - if you get a bad entry, and the trend does continue, you might still be correct in the market movement in the long term, but you will face very large drawdowns for a longer period of time, where the price will have probably already have hit your stop loss.

Image 53: The Moving Average filtering out bearish trade positions, due the bullish moving average on the hourly CAD/JPY.

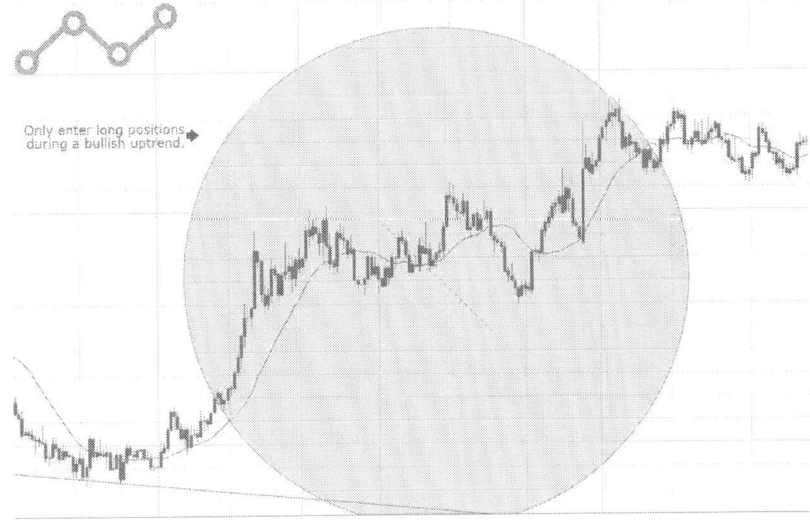

Moving Average Crossovers

Crossovers are probably one of the most popular trading strategies used by new traders, as they implement indicators and seem simple yet advanced enough to make a profitable strategy to beginner traders.

A popular trend following strategy, consisting of entering a trade in the direction of a small period moving average "crossing over" with a larger period moving average; as it represents the most recent price movements moving against the long term average and can indicate important price turnarounds.

Image 54: The Moving Average crossovers predicting market movements on the hourly USOIL chart.

However, these trades are often inaccurate due to the crossovers often being initiated due to economic news, and the trading pair just having a pullback - creating a fake signal as the trend then retraces and moves in the original direction.

Due to these factors, we do not recommend using any type of crossover as they provide inconsistent trading signals and don't provide take profit or stop loss levels.

Dynamic Support and Resistance

Moving averages should mostly be used as a confluence factor for pairs that are in a clear trend - you should refrain from using a volatile moving average setting when pairs are in a flat channel as this will not provide clear or accurate signals.

Image 55: The 50 period moving average acting as a dynamic resistance on the 4 hour Euro to Great Britain Pound chart.

Generally, entering with the use of a moving average should only be done when the price reaches the moving average line as a "retest" - meaning it is trending, and by reaching the moving average level, traders countertrading the trend are satisfied with their profit, close out their positions and new traders can enter in the direction of the original trend.

Upon having entered a trade upon the retest, a stop loss can be placed above or below the moving average at a reasonable distance to ensure that the price is not just consolidating and stops you out while trading a lower time frame range.

Distinguishing Between MA Types

There are four main types of Moving Average available to the most basic retail traders on most platforms; the Simple MA, Exponential MA, Smoothed MA and the Linear Weighted MA.

However, the most popular ones by far are the Simple and Exponential - and due to their popularity, it is not advised to use the other two types as you want to be trading with the majority of other traders and so using the same tools will let you make informed trading decisions.

The difference between these two moving averages is a difference in the mathematical calculation from the price used to represent in a single line. Due to the math behind it, the

EMA respects the most recent candlesticks more heavily than the SMA because the SMA respects all candlesticks in the predetermined range equally and so the EMA is quicker and more volatile to react to sudden price changes which is more beneficial to scalpers, and shorter term traders.

This means that moving averages overall are incredibly flexible to be able to be used for both long term traders and short term traders - this does however mean that there are some disadvantages with both types of moving average.

Image 56: The hourly Great Britain Pound to Japanese Yen displaying the difference between the EMA and SMA.

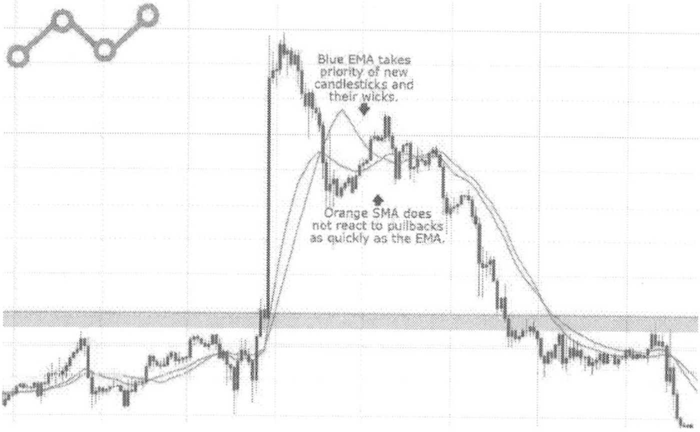

For instance, if a trader focuses heavily on the reaction of the EMA, a quick pullback or stop hunt from large "whales" will ensure that the trader has exited their position at a poor position, with only a percentage of possible profits.

This is also true for the other direction, if using a SMA it is probable that a trader will react very slowly and not get a good entry position when a pair begins a new trend.

Therefore, there is no definitive answer to the best moving average type - but instead depends on the quality of the trader and their trading style.

Setting up Moving Averages

Another important factor of moving averages, are the period settings which were covered lightly previously.

A vital detail about making this decision relies on the overall type of trader you are - for example by being a longer term trader, such as a swing trader you will not pay much attention to smaller market movements like corrections and should therefore choose a less reactive/volatile moving average setting - unlike a scalper who is paying constant attention and wants to maximise profits from early entries and exits; who will benefit more from a smaller period setting on their MA.

Moving Average Presets

100-200 Period Setting

These settings are the swing trading extremities, with very slow reactions and smooth appearance. They will often be used for long term investing and are also seen often in newspapers or financial TV - which amplifies the strength of them due to the majority of traders trading using these settings.

Image 57: The 100 period moving average rarely changing directions on the daily Swiss Franc to Japanese Yen.

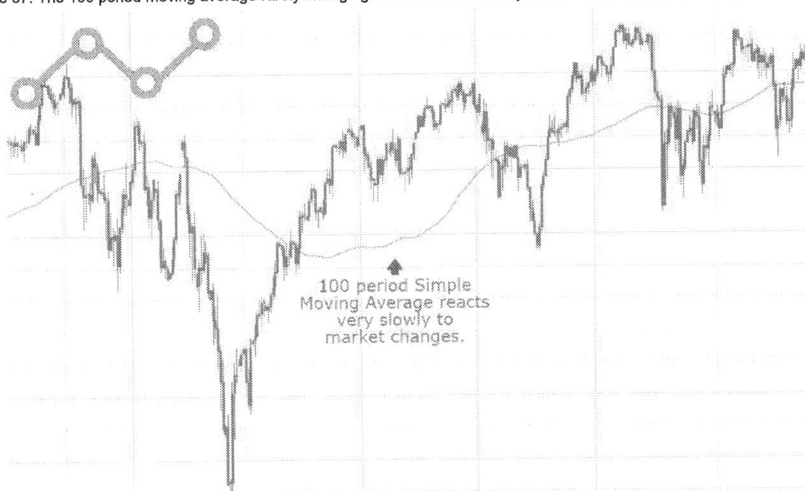

They can be used as very trustworthy dynamic support and resistance zones, as they act as targets for traders and levels for pending orders - which means there will almost always be a large or small reaction once the price reaches the moving average.

50 Period Setting

The 50 period setting MA is similar to the 100-200 period settings, however it is probably even more popular. It provides a nice middle ground to sudden price changes due to economic activity but still allows long term swing traders to use it's levels for algorithmic trading due to it being quite slow.

Once again, this setting can be used as a support and resistance zone; however requires more confluence factors to fully support a trading decision unlike the 100-200 period settings, as their signals are more rare but often more accurate.

Image 58: The 50 period moving average following the hourly Canadian Dollar to Japanese Yen very accurately.

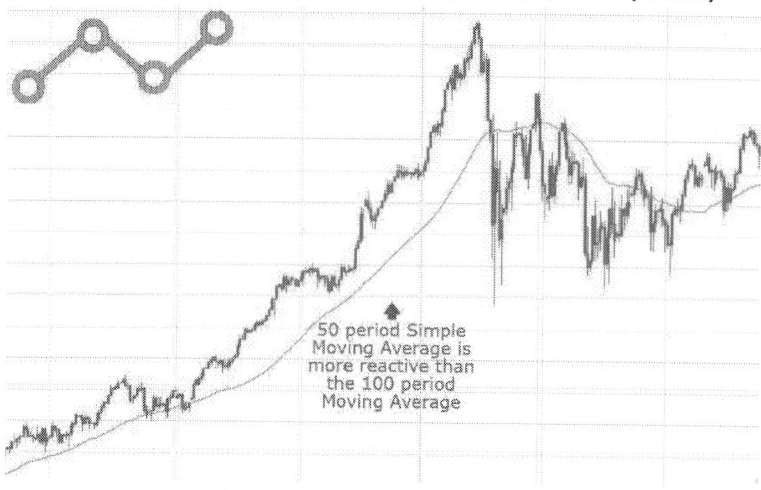

21 Period Setting

This period setting is considered a medium term period setting, and is recommended for day trading on the hourly or 4 hour timeframe - swing trading should be kept to the higher period settings.

This setting will react moderately quickly to sudden price changes and can be used for scalpers that are reserved, and not aggressive enough to use even lower period settings.

Image 59: The 21 period moving average reacting to major pullbacks on the 4 hour USOIL chart.

This setting is also a part of the Fibonacci Number sequence, and so this popularised the setting as some traders are very traditional and believe heavily in the importance of Fibonnaci numbers in trading.

9-10 Period Setting

These settings are also very popular, due to their extended use from very risk taking scalpers, that trade on very low timeframes and focus on small corrections and pullbacks - this is because these settings react very quickly to any price changes.

Image 60: The 9 period moving average reacting quickly to corrections on the hourly gold (XAU/USD) chart.

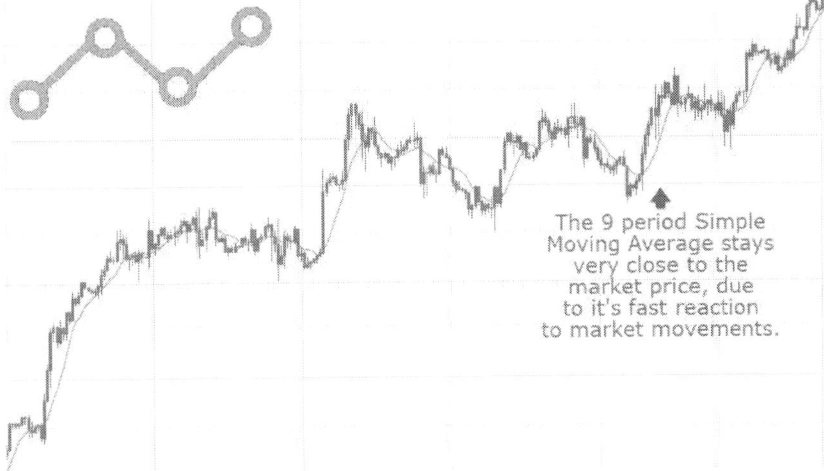

We personally do not recommend the use of these settings, due to their inability to react accordingly to economic changes and are often trumped by general higher timeframe price action analysis, meaning that all short term scalps will not always result profitably.

Relative Strength Index (R.S.I)

Relative Strength Index is an indicator developed by Welles Wilder to assess the strength or weakness of the current price movements measures the volatility of price changes by comparing price increases with its losses over a certain period.

The RSI indicator is likely the second most popular indicator among all levels of traders, due to the versatility and accuracy of the indicator - it is clear that it provides another level of confluence and acts as a good entry indicator; due to some level of reaction happening.

Image 61: The RSI indicator displaying current market information on the daily US30 chart.

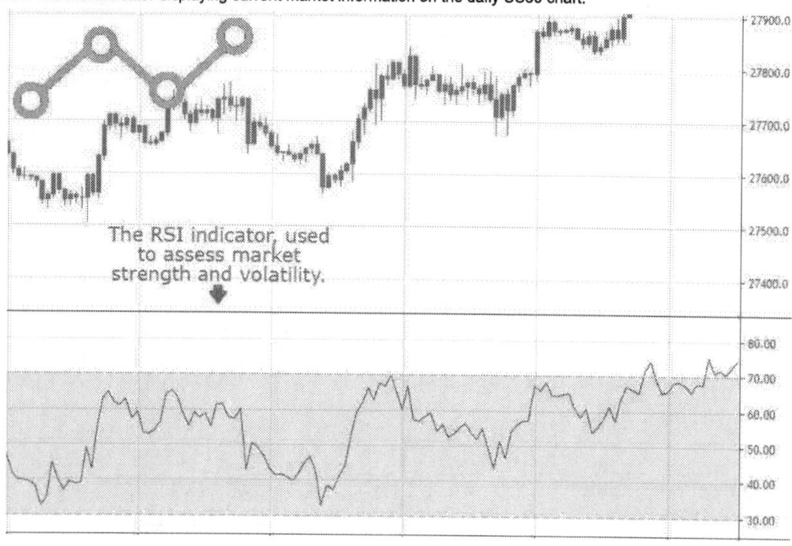

Construction of the RSI

The RSI sums up the total upwards price movement in the last predetermined number of candlesticks and compares it to the total downward movement presented by the price in the same candlestick range; therefore the RSI acts as a ratio of price movements.

The number of candlesticks that are taken into the calculation can be changed by changing the period of the RSI - however, it is recommended that to comply with the trading decisions made by the majority of traders, that you stick with a period of 14.

RSI Signals

"Oversold" and "Overbought"

The RSI value can be distinguished between being "Oversold" and "Overbought" when the calculation results in less than 30 or more than 70, respectively.

This does often result in beginner traders assuming that once the price exceeds these values, that the trend is over and the price is about to reverse. There is some truth to this, as a high or low RSI value means the market has been very one sided for the past selected amount of candlesticks, and there is likely a small pullback foreboding, or a consolidation phase to bring the RSI back to neutral levels of around 50.

Image 62: The overbought levels on the RSI displayed on the hourly US30 chart.

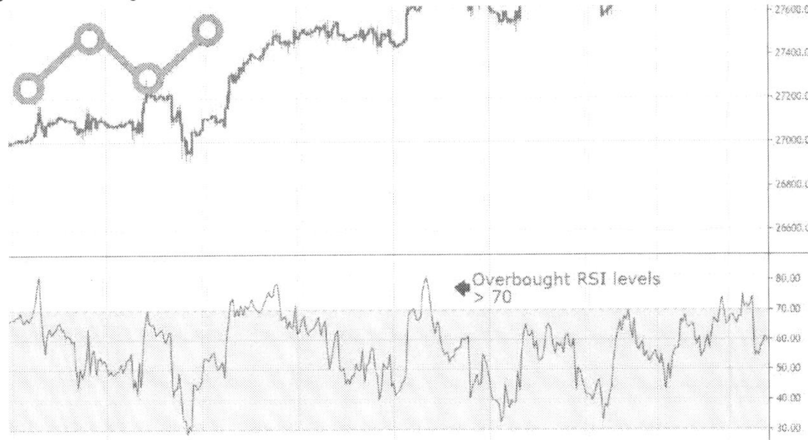

However, these pullbacks or retracements are not strong enough indications to enter the market, as they can be incredibly small if there are no other confluence factors acting against the trend.

This does go against the belief of many beginner traders, due to the poor selection of words used to describe these values by Welles Wilder and should be seen as "Very Strong Uptrend" and "Very Strong Downtrend" instead of "Overbought" and "Oversold".

This separation should be made, due to the possibility of traders seeing (for example) a good bullish price action setup to the upside, but refrain from entering due to RSI already being at "Overbought" levels - where in reality this can be a positive confluence factor as it shows high momentum to the upside is already present, and so in this scenario the trader should wait for the small retracement from the RSI and enter at a better price to result in a highly profitable trade.

The same can be applied to a wide range of scenarios, such as a breakout of a trading range being supported by an already extreme RSI value showing that the momentum and trend is already underway.

RSI Dynamic Support & Resistance

Due to the RSI calculating a ratio between the positive price movements and negative price movements, it is possible to use the RSI levels as support and resistance zones as described before in this trading manual.

By recognising a RSI level where price often tends to reverse in the current market conditions, you can take advantage of that and construct accurate market setups with those key levels in mind.

Image 63: The US30 4 hour chart displays a dynamic resistance of 63 in this market phase.

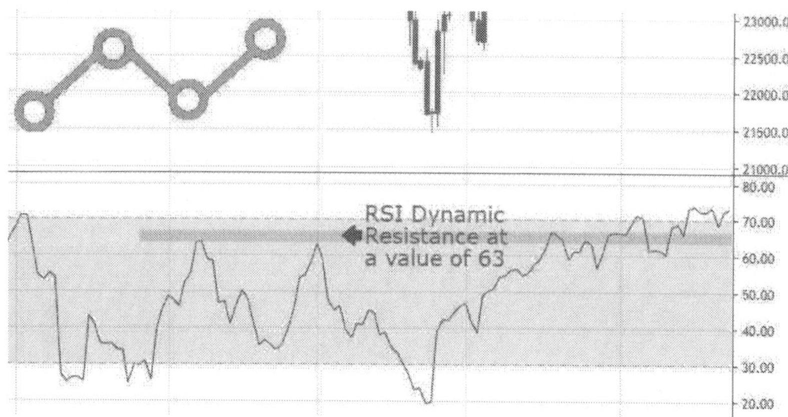

For example, if the RSI continually peaks at a value of 60, and then reverses, an upwards channel might be present with the price reaching the upper ascending trend line at the same points that the RSI is at a value of 60 - if so, this information can be used to better inform a trading decision for the future; for either when the price reaches the trend line again, an RSI of 60 or both.

RSI Divergence

The RSI Divergence is undoubtedly our preferred method of analysing the market using the RSI, due to its accuracy and the very large potential risk reward ratio when used correctly because of the forthcoming market volatility that it represents.

The Divergence signal occurs when the market price has swing highs and swing lows that differ from the RSI representation - for example, when the market price has its first swing high, with an RSI value of 75; then the market retraces and corrects to then eventually create a higher swing high yet again, but with a RSI level of only 65.

This market condition represents a difference ("Divergence") between the trendline price action created by the market and the trend line represented by the RSI.

This means that the most recent market swing has reached new levels in these market conditions, but the underlying market movements mean that this swing was weaker than the previous swing high and the trend cannot continue for much longer.

Therefore, a strong shift between bulls and bears is about to take place - and this last impulse in the market forebodes a strong market movement in the opposite direction, which can be taken advantage of.

Image 64: RSI Divergence clearly shown prior to a small bearish rally on the hourly New Zealand Dollar to Canadian Dollar.

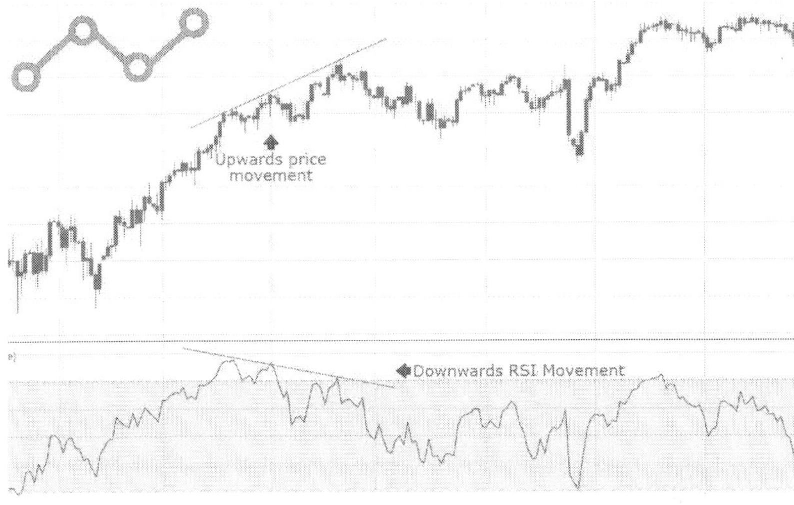

The Stochastic Indicator

The Stochastic Indicator is useful in quickly discerning the speed and strength of the market movements by providing knowledge about momentum and trend strength.

Image 65: The stochastic indicator displaying market speed and strength on the daily Australian Dollar to Swiss Franc.

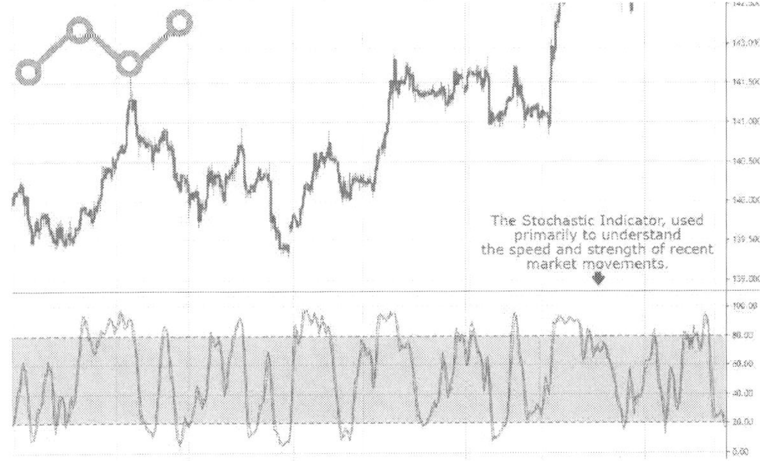

Jonas Navardauskas
Owner of .4x Team

Often, a longer term trend on higher time frames does not reverse instantly - in the matter of one or two candles; because a previous trend must first stop its bullish or bearish momentum to then get absorbed by the opposite market participants and a new trend can form in the opposite direction. This is what George Lane (the creator of the Stochastic Indicator) had meant with his famous "rocket slowing down before changing direction" metaphor.

Construction of the Stochastic

The Stochastic take a range, similar to an RSI and is most often used with periods of 5 or 14 - which accounts the last 5 or 14 candlesticks.

This indicator works by taking the absolute low of the predetermined candlestick range and also taking into account the absolute high in the same range - and then uses these values to compare it to the current price and give a percentage or value between 0 and 100, once again similar to the Relative Strength Index.

This indicator therefore represents very similar information to the RSI, as both are oscillating momentum indicators.

Stochastic Signals

"Oversold" vs "Overbought"

Once again, it is important to touch upon the misrepresentation of the statements "Oversold" and "Overbought", as already mentioned in the RSI chapter.

Image 66: The key stochastic zones displayed on the daily Great Britain Pound to Japanese Yen chart.

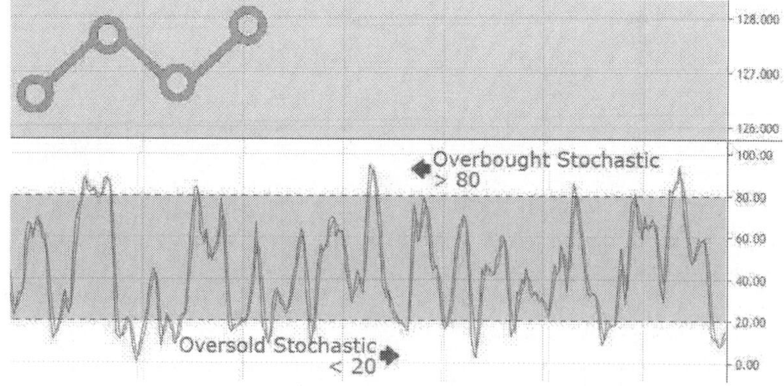

Jonas Navardauskas
Owner of .4x Team

The Stochastic Indicator determines values above 80, as Overbought and below 20 as Oversold - but this once again does not represent or forebode any market reversal and instead means that the market is in a strong position with high momentum.

Breakout Signals

With a Stochastic moving quickly and strongly near an extreme percentage value, and the two Stochastic bands separating - this shows traders that a change in market direction is to be expected.

By the Stochastic moving violently, it means that the price is at an extreme of the last predetermined range of candlesticks and the trend is gaining a lot of momentum - this Stochastic pattern should be accompanied by a breakout or rejection from a supply or demand zone to create a valid trade idea and should not be used on its own, but instead as a strong confluence factor.

Image 67: Large bullish market rally with a constantly "Overbought" stochastic level on the 4 hour Euro to Japanese Yen.

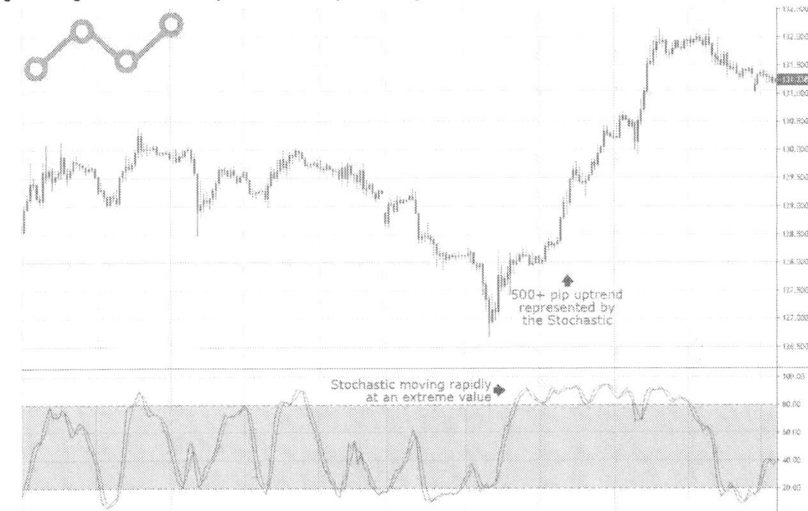

Trend Following Signals

By having a Stochastic continuing in one direction, and an agreeing market price action analysis - it is alright to enter the market and "chase" the market trend, due to it being very difficult to trade against the Stochastic, therefore using it to your advantage and remaining in the trade longer is the correct decision.

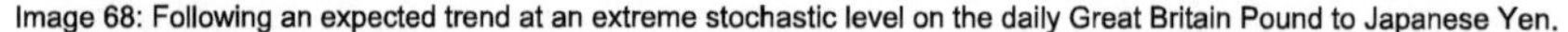

Image 68: Following an expected trend at an extreme stochastic level on the daily Great Britain Pound to Japanese Yen.

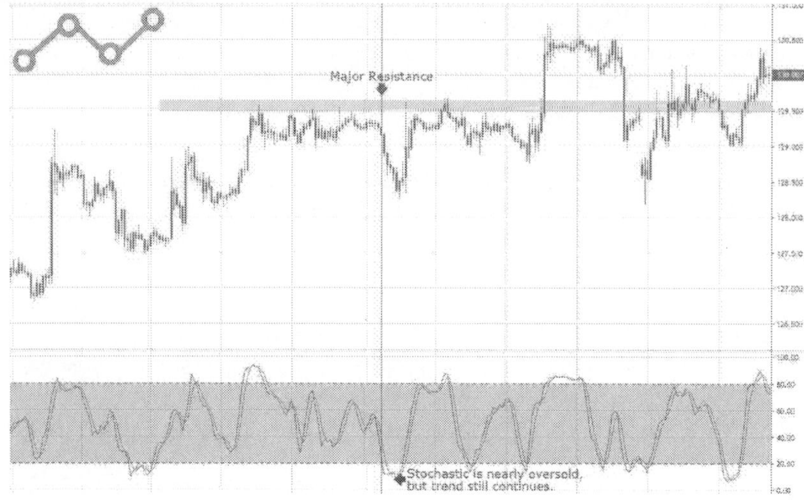

This idea can also be used even when the Stochastic is at extreme "Oversold" and "Overbought" levels, due to the previous explanation of it representing a very strong trend with large momentum, which is difficult to stop without economic factors or strong supply or demand zones.

Stochastic Divergence

The Stochastic Divergence is incredibly important, due to the massive market movements it can indicate before they actually happen.

The Divergence is created when the stochastic's highs or lows are misrepresented by the swing lows and swing highs shown by the price in the market - meaning that even though the price is at relatively unseen levels in the last realistic trading range, the Stochastic represents it as a weak movement, and shows an underlying lack of bullish or bearish momentum to propel the price to new levels.

If there is not enough momentum in one direction after a series of higher or lower peaks, it is likely that the trend following traders are contempt with their profit and close out, meaning they open an opposite position which creates price absorption by the opposite market participants and produces market movements just as volatile, or even more rapid in the opposite direction.

Image 69: A Stochastic divergence prior to a market sell-off on the 4 hour US30 chart.

Bollinger Bands

Bollinger Bands are an indicator that combines different types of indicators into one, and is therefore incredibly versatile when used correctly in trading.

Image 70: The Bollinger Bands indicator displaying market volatility on the 4 hour Euro to Japanese Yen chart.

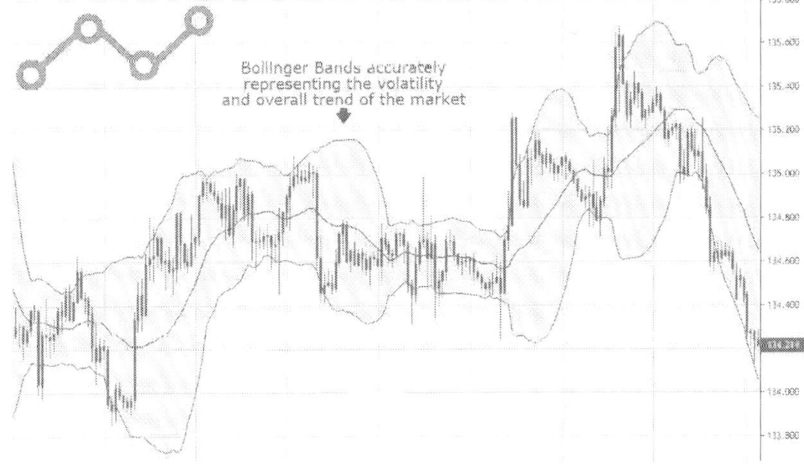

Jonas Navardauskas
Owner of .4x Team

By being able to identify the volatility and the overall trend of the market at once makes the Bollinger Bands a commonly used short term and medium term trading tool, and often many beginner traders only use this one indicator, and are relatively successful while the market conditions are correct for using it.

Construction of the Bollinger Bands

Bollinger Bands are formed with the use of a inter-median channel, created by two outer lines/bands that accurately represent the volatility of the market, with the bands expanding when the market is noticeably volatile, and compressing/squeezing together if the market is at a standstill or consolidating.

The middle band of the Bollinger Bands is a moving average, usually with a period of 20 - but can be changed to accommodate for shorter term traders or longer term traders, as mentioned in the Moving Averages chapter.

The two outer volatility bands are calculated using standard deviations from the price itself, and usually have a deviation setting of 2, but can be changed depending on the amount of false signals received due to the timeframe used and false signals created due to the noise of the market breathing.

Image 71: The construction and key components of the Bollinger Bands on the hourly Euro to Japanese Yen.

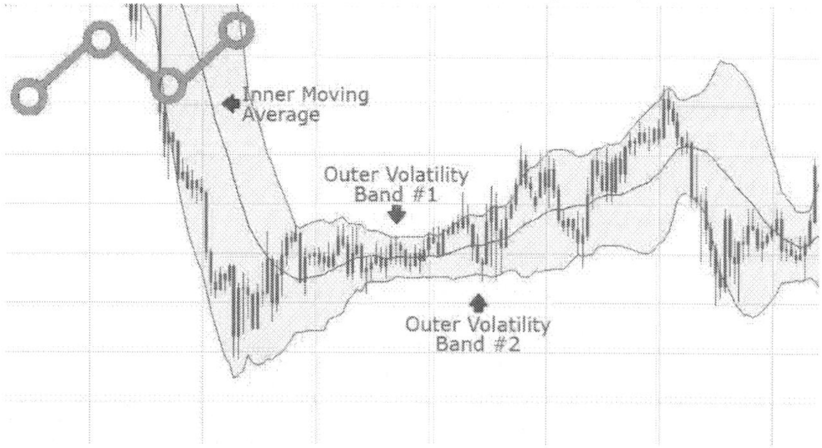

Bollinger Bands Signals

Trend Following using Bollinger Bands

Bollinger Bands are designed for the use of trend following trading.

This is because during strong trending phases of the market, the price often moves along the outside volatility bands and therefore represents a strong market direction if there is continual movement near the edge of the channel.

On the other hand, when the price moves back to the middle band (the moving average) this means the trend is weakening or retracing - if the price then continues past the middle band and breaks it, this signals the end of the prevailing trend.

When the price is moving alongside the outer channel and is therefore displaying a strong market direction, it is recommended to wait for a retracement or pullback to the middle band, instead of entering instantly and possibly getting an unforgiving entry.

Once the price has reached the middle Bollinger Band, it is important to wait for agreeing price action at this level to enter a new position and it is expected for the market to then continue along the outer channel of the Bollinger band.

Image 72: The 4 hour US Dollar to Canadian Dollar clearly respecting and retesting the inner moving average.

By maintaining a stop loss above or below the middle band, depending on the market direction, it is unlikely that you exit your position too early - because once the market has moved outside of one side of the Bollinger Bands and moves past the moving average, the prevailing market phase is over and new trading decisions need to be found.

Reversal Trading using Bollinger Bands

Due to the Bollinger Bands being designed for trend following traders, it is very rare that the Bollinger Bands create a reversal signal but it should still be taken into account when it does.

A possible reversal trend signals created by the Bollinger Bands is when the market is moving alongside the outer band, and a strong impulse movement pushes the price outside of the outer Bollinger Band, but does not close outside and instead creates a price action rejection trade that can be taken in the opposite direction of the prevailing trend - due to the outer Bollinger Band acting as a key level that the market cannot push past.

Image 73: The hourly Canadian Dollar to Japanese Yen market recovering after a wick retest of the outside volatility band.

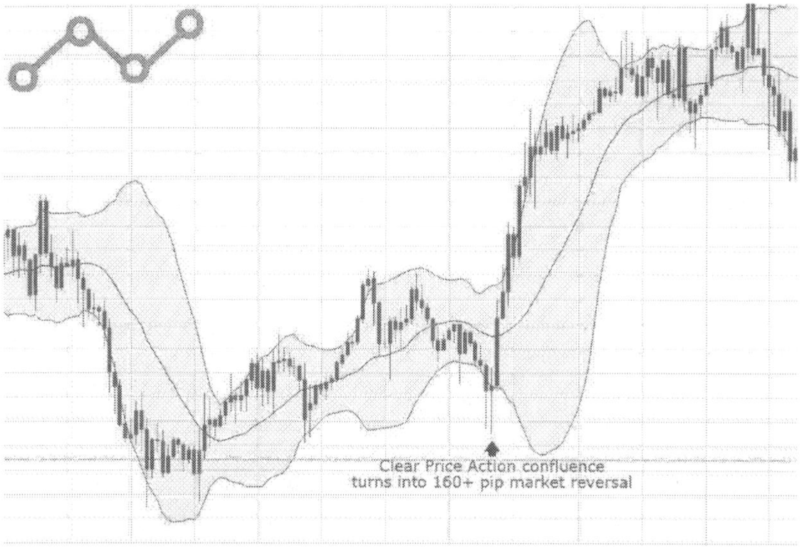

MACD

The MACD indicator is another incredibly popular trading tool, with versatile uses and ability to identify momentum and trends.

This versatility is due to the basis of the MACD being multiple moving averages to represent trends, and a bar chart used to identify market volume and momentum.

Image 74: The MACD indicator used on a daily gold (XAU/USD) chart.

Construction of the MACD

The MACD stands for Moving Average Convergence Divergence indicator, and consists of three components: one to represent the convergence of the market sentiment, another one to represent the market volume by calculating divergence, and finally a moving average.

Convergence (MACD) Line

This is the most important factor of the indicator, and the most advanced.

By calculating the difference between a 12 period moving average and 26 period moving average, it can represent the overall market trend due to it covering both short term movements (with a 12 period MA) and longer term price changes (due to the 26 period MA).

This therefore means that the MACD line presents the trend changes, strength and direction accurately, as it utilises different timeframes to decide an overall market sentiment.

"Signal" Line

The Signal line is represented as a quicker reacting line, next to the MACD line, but is often more accurate during sudden market movements - due to the default period setting being 9, making it more useful in shorter term trading using the MACD indicator. and scalping

By taking advantage of a moving average crossover system with the MACD line and combining it with a fast and popular moving average; the indicator allows traders to correctly inform themselves about all short term price shifts and get good market entries or exits if already in a trading position.

Volume Chart

The volume chart visible at the bottom of the MACD indicator represents the market volume and momentum by calculating a divergence.

This is done by working out the difference in value between the previously mentioned MACD line and Signal line - as the Signal line is a faster reacting line than the MACD line, the representation of the current difference between these two components creates an accurate indication of current market momentum and volume being traded.

Image 75: The key components of the MACD labelled on the hourly Canadian Dollar to Japanese Yen.

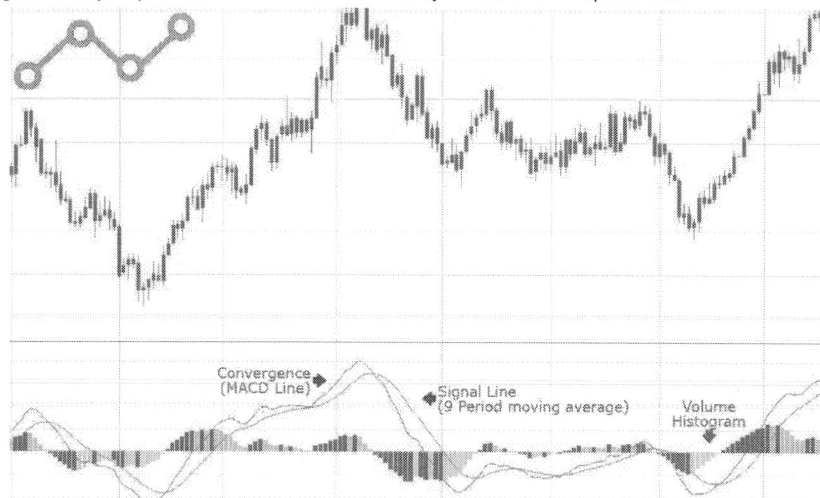

MACD Signals

Buy and Sell Triggers

The use of trading triggers from the signal line should be restricted to when the two lines (MACD line and Signal line) are parting and continue to distance away from one another - this represents a high market momentum and a high overall strength of the market.

When combining this understanding with the volume bar chart, it is very easy to discern between good entry opportunities and when you should refrain from creating a trading position, due to low market movement.

By waiting for the market to reach an extreme level inside the MACD indicator, and then entering when the MACD provides a crossover of the MACD line and signal line, you are increasing your trade success probability, due to a fast crossover representing a strong and sudden market impulse - which can continue for a while if this analysis is used as a confluence factor for general price action analysis.

Image 76: Two possible trading positions influenced by the MACD on the daily Great Britain Pound to Australian Dollar.

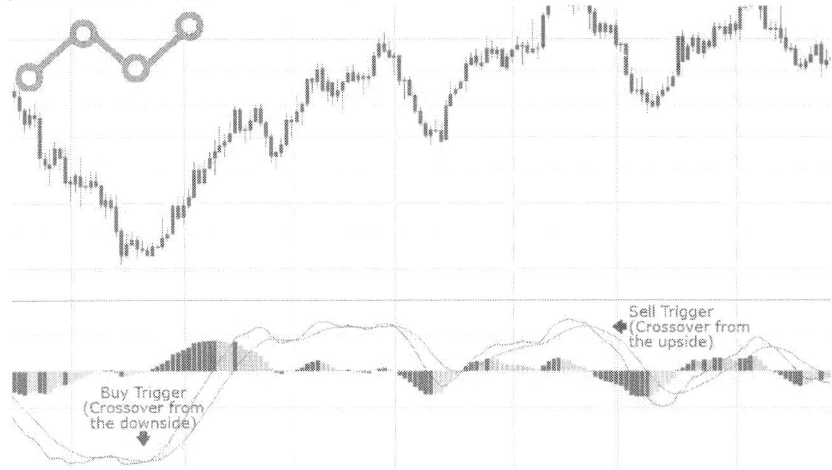

When the MACD crosses above the signal line, you can know that the market sentiment has shifted from bearish to bullish.

MACD Divergence

The divergence from the MACD indicator is often very effective when combined with price action analysis - as it can show an underlying weakness in the overall trend, similar to the RSI and Stochastic divergences, indicating a possible high volatility market reversal.

Image 77: The MACD divergence used to analyse a small market sell-off on the hourly Australian Dollar to Swiss Franc.

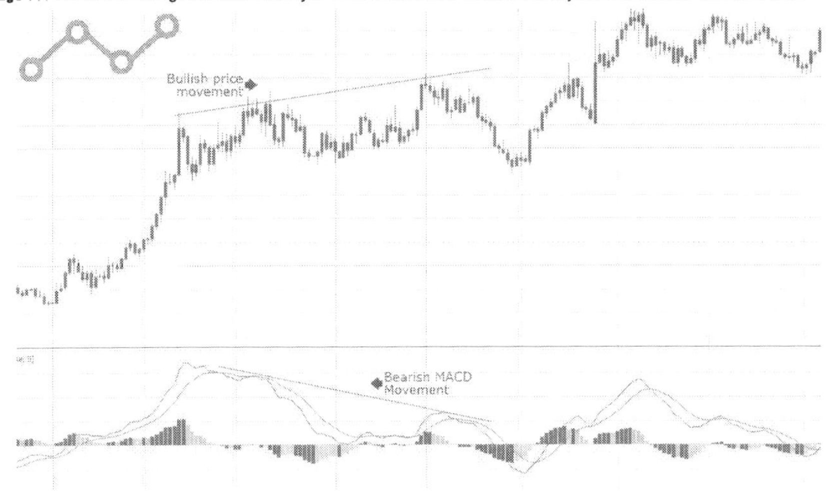

For example, by using the MACD and being able to see that a continuation of higher and higher highs or lower and lower lows are misrepresented by the MACD indicator, a trader can be significantly better informed (in comparison to other traders) about the low probability that a trend following position will become profitable.

Because of the MACD opposing the general market direction of the price; shown by the candlesticks, it proves that the trend is weakening and it is unlikely to continue. Therefore it is correct to patiently wait for a potential reversal trading position in the opposite direction of the prevailing trend, which will result in a notably higher risk to reward ratio trade.

Further Technical Analysis Fragments

From reading the previous chapters in this trading manual - you should already be able to recognise possible market formations and movements if they're formed exactly "textbook", however this is never the case and it is more important for you to be able to create your own additional charting segments such as the support and resistance zones, trend lines, breakouts and possible market traps.

Trend Lines

A trend line as a concept is incredibly simple, and should always be seen as this. There are often traders I've spoken to that struggle to decide the overall trend of a market.

It should be looked at as if a 5 year old is looking at the market: "Oh, it's going down/up".
I personally do not advocate calculating each higher high or lower low, when deciding the market movement, as other traders do because the market is never perfect and an overall market consensus should be easily recognised.

There is a chance that if you are struggling to discern the overall trend - you are just overcomplicating it all.

Constructing Trend Lines

A trend line represents multiple market swings at the same angle from the previous major market swing.

This is done simply by joining each swing low in an uptrend and each swing high in a downtrend.

However, for a valid trend line to appear, there must be three valid connections to the swings of a market.

They should not be well into the candle body and should have a consistent point across all highs/lows by connecting either the extreme body price or the extreme wick price. Any trend line that cannot form three clear, obvious connections should be avoided as they will produce fake signals. It is better to not create a trend line, than to create a bad or invalid one.

Image 78: Ascending trend line becomes valid after the 2nd touch on the daily EURNZD chart.

Using Trend Lines

In our opinion, trend lines are one of the most vital chart concepts that exist. This is because they are universally used by scalpers, day traders, swing traders and everything in between.

With the correct ability, they can be used both for trend traders and reversal traders - as they can be used as horizontal support/resistance zones; therefore all the same rules apply, such as depending on price action confluence, clear breakouts, retests e.t.c.

It is not always advisable to use a trend line signal formation as soon as it appears - this is often if the trend line angle is at an extreme (e.g very steep, or the opposite: very shallow). This is because, from personal experience, it is often unsustainable and can create volatile movements in the opposite direction of the trend line signal generated.

This, however, is quite subjective and depends on your personal trading style. As a more aggressive trader, you can enter a position at the appearance of an extremely steep trend line, and maintain a close stop loss in profit to ensure some profit remains locked in - but this requires constant attention due to, as previously mentioned, these breakouts often being unsustainable and captures the greed of other traders who are attempting to catch some of the movement.

On the other hand, you can remain a reserved trader and only take trades where the angle is more reasonable - from around 20 degrees to 70 degrees. This will ensure you are not entering a market that is moving too quickly and causes emotional actions from other traders.

Image 79: An appropriate trend line angle on the daily Gold chart, with the angle between 20 degrees and 70 degrees.

Breaks of Trend-Lines

As traders, we are not expected to know what will happen at a price zone - but instead we have to wait and see how the price will react once it reaches that area. Often, with a trend line it is expected to react and be rejected by the trend line; however, if the trend line is broken through with very little or no stalling then a strong trading signal is created.

This break in the trend line (depending on the previous strength of the trend line) can represent a complete market shift and a change in market structure.

The break of a trend line will always be represented by a failure of the market to make a higher high or a lower low and present a new trend.

Image 80: No market reaction presented at the trend line, and therefore creates a new market structure on the hourly GBPJPY.

Support and Resistance

Support and resistance zones and levels are by far the most important aspect of forex trading.

I am confident that with enough manual backtesting and practice, any trader can easily become profitable by keeping it simple and monitoring price action around the strongest zones and waiting for price reactions.

Support and resistance zones are almost always respected and can be trusted - however, can always be trumped by major fundamental news releases, and traders must be constantly wary of this in their market analysis.

Price swings in the majority of stocks and shares market is not as important as it is in the foreign exchange market.

We already know the fact that the market can be profitable due to the majority of institutions and large "whales" always trading in similar patterns - often from support and resistance levels.

However, smaller market users such as you and us all participate in the overall market fluctuation on a smaller price level. This is why things such as corrections and market swings happen very often.

A large mental breakthrough for many traders is the understanding that when a user is in a "Long" position (a buy) - and they are happy with their profit, they must close the trade - when you close a "Long" position, you have to (in theory) open up a "Short" position.

Image 81: Support and Resistance zones broken due to economic news on the hourly Great Britain Pound to Australian Dollar.

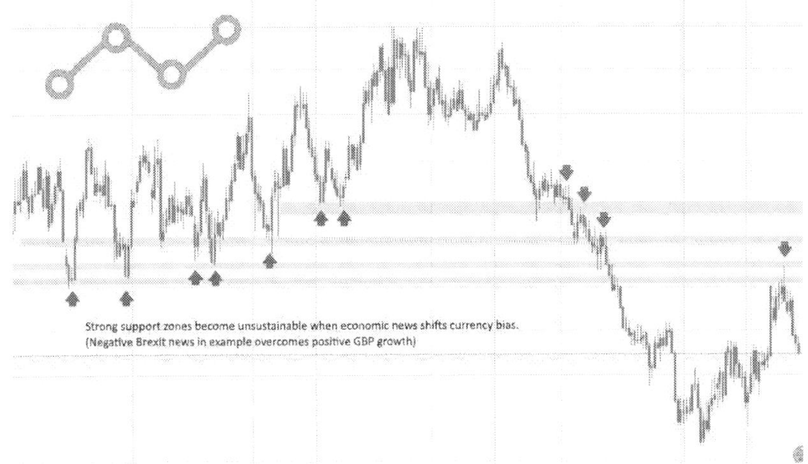

This is the main reason why previous support and resistance levels tend to work so often.

As a trader buys at the bottom of a "box" range, and closes the position at the top of the "box" range, they are in essence opening up a sell position to counteract their earlier buy and therefore securing their profit.

When hundreds of thousands of traders all see this same opportunity - that is what creates these support and resistance zones.

Constructing Support and Resistance

Our method of presenting support and resistance levels is not the most popular and often questioned.

I believe that any price reaction on the higher time-frames must be marked and presented as a support or resistance zone.

Once you begin doing this automatically on every chart you see, it is very impressive just how many times the price reacts to zones and therefore trading and predicting market movement becomes significantly easier.

Simply put, a resistance zone is a peak for a certain period of market movement. This is where market rally has come to a consolidation or rejection and has not advanced past.

On the other hand, a support zone is the opposite and is where a market sell off has finished and therefore been rejected and began an uptrend.

Image 82: Support and Resistance flip zones labelled on the daily USOIL Chart.

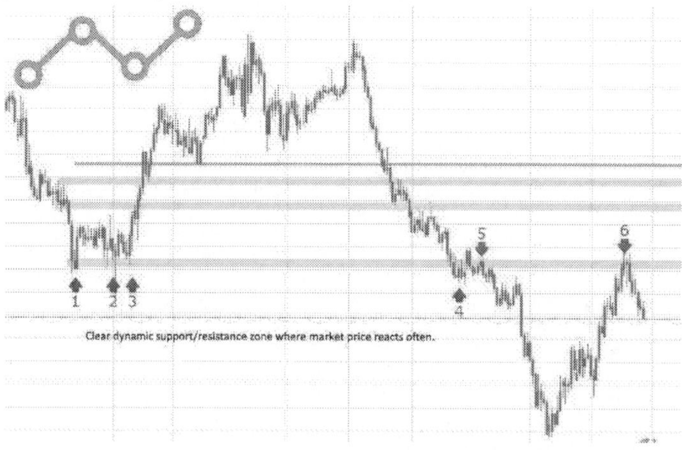

Similar to trend lines, support and resistance zones can be considered weak or strong - and the more reactions at a certain price, the stronger the zone is.

The Theory Behind Support & Resistance

As mentioned earlier in the manual, trading depends on other traders making the same decisions and conclusions as you - which is why having a large number of confluence factors assist you in trading due to each factor being a possible analysis point from other traders.

Image 83: A Support level labelled on the 4 hour Canadian Dollar to Japanese Yen with 6 retests.

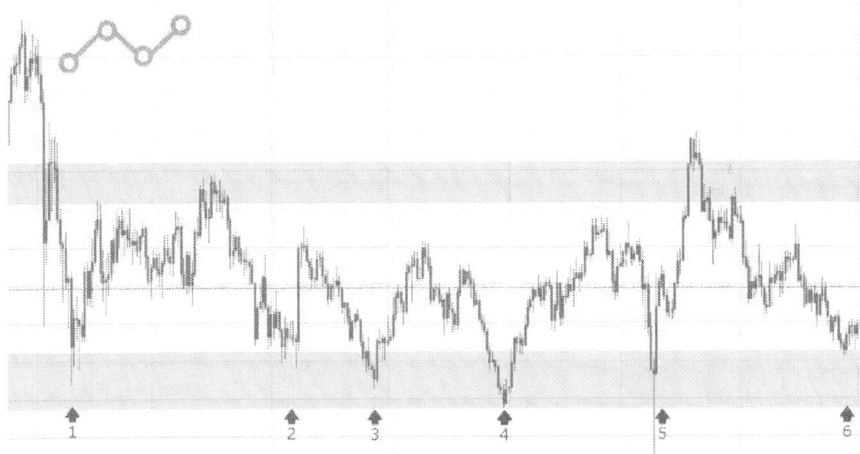

When the price of a currency pair continuously reacts to a support zone, the number of sellers and buyers changes - and is universally decided a price where the traders in short positions are contempt with their profit, and close their trades and vice-versa where bullish traders go long as the price is in theory "cheap" enough to enter and therefore causes a change in market trend and momentum.

Trading using Support & Resistance

A key idea that many traders fail to realise about support and resistance levels are that they are not direct price numbers, but instead act as a "zone" where the orders of other traders get absorbed.

This does, however, create some variance as it is unsure whether the change of a market trend is close enough to the other rejections to be considered in the same "zone" - but this decision-making comes with experience and expertise in the market pairs.

Image 84: A key resistance "zone" labelled on the daily Euro to US Dollar chart.

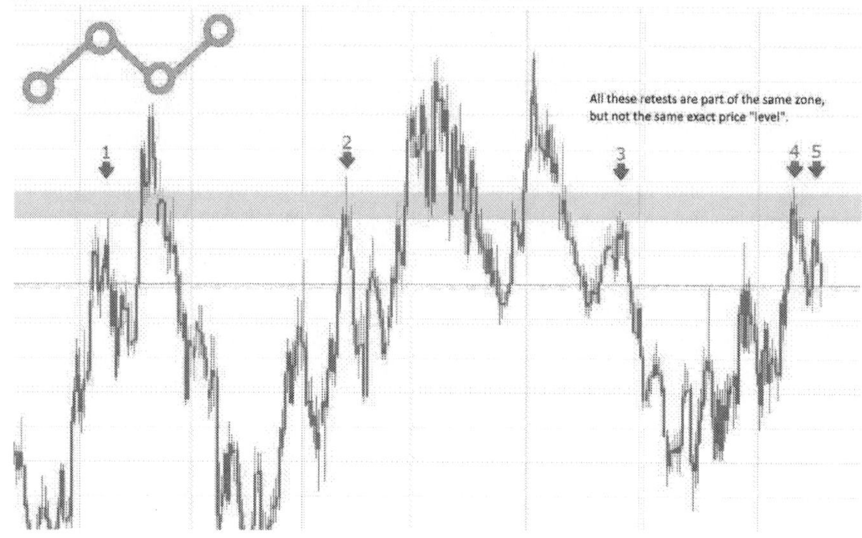

As well as this, trading by support and resistance only is not advised - but should be instead used as an incredibly strong confluence factor and should not be traded blindly when the price approaches a prior zone because if there is no appropriate market reaction presented in the candles - then it might be a clear breakout or large financial traders "stop-hunting" other traders.

Image 85: An additional Head & Shoulders formation is a confluence factor for the hourly gold (XAUUSD) chart.

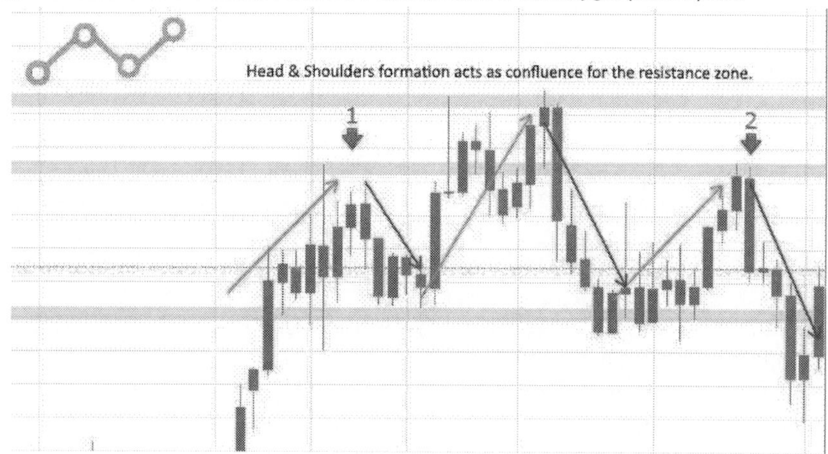

Development of Support and Resistance Zones

The same as everything, support and resistance zones are not perfect and eventually break down and cannot be relied on. This is because traders eventually like to become greedy and do not want to stick to the same trades between zones and instead enter for potentially larger moves, such as breakouts and volatile movements.

This means that each time the price eventually reaches a previous resistance - there are less traders selling, and more traders attempting to shift the market bias and going long to encourage a breakout.

Image 86: The reactions weaken and eventually the support breaks on the daily Canadian Dollar to Japanese Yen.

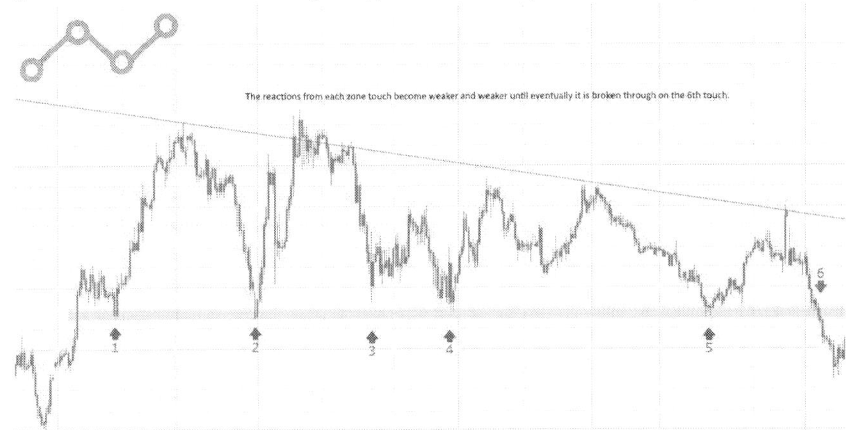

Eventually, when enough traders think like this (and often boosted by some fundamental, economic news) then the price does break through and encourages a whole new market phase where trading ideas need to be reviewed.

This is dangerous because traders that are complying with the previous market movements between zones often receive an accurate entry and are in profit - but because each market swing becomes smaller and smaller, prior to the eventual breakout, then there is no predetermined take profit level and instead needs to be monitored and decisions need to be made with purely price action in mind on when to exit.

Supply and Demand

Supply and Demand zones are nearly the same as support and resistance zones and also are used the same in trading - but feature some significant differences that means they can both be used in conjunction to determine accurate and major price levels.

Supply and Demand vs Support and Resistance

As mentioned earlier, these two chart analysis features are similar but Supply and Demand zones are used to describe a often smaller support/resistance zone with a significantly stronger reaction - which means many trading orders where waiting at this exact price level to enter, or it was a level used by larger traders and financial institutions because the ratio of buyers is significantly different to the ratio of sellers and therefore creates the sudden explosion in price.

Image 87: A clear supply zone presented on the daily US30 chart, due to fast and strong reactions from it.

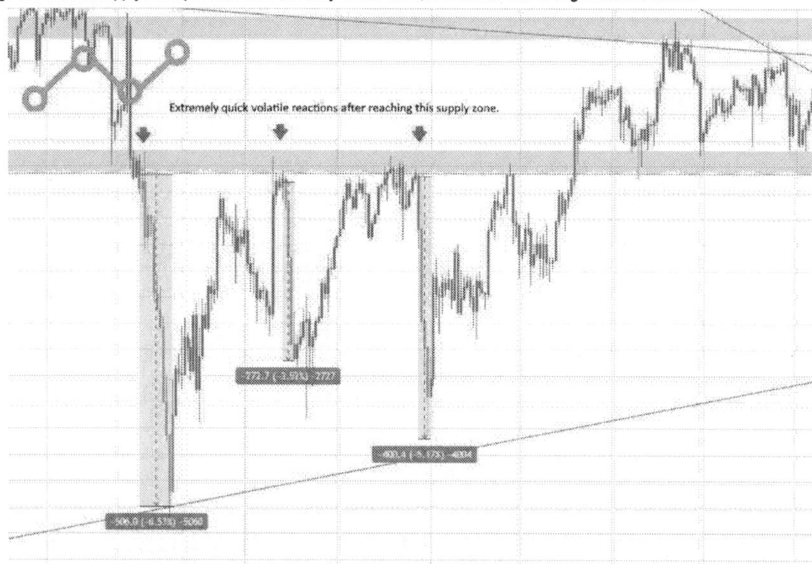

The reason that supply and demand zones continue to exist after the first volatile market movement, is because many traders did not participate in the first market movement, and are now waiting for the price to reach this level again and are expecting a similar movement and so many trade orders are waiting at this exact zone, which can be taken advantage of.

Constructing Supply and Demand Zones

Supply and Demand zones differ from the usual Supply and Resistance zones, by only working and providing orders in one direction - the zones cannot “flip” like mentioned earlier with Support and Resistance.

Therefore, it is easier to construct supply and demand zones and there are a few key elements that cannot be forgotten:

- ### Strong Breakout

The most important aspect of determining a supply or demand zone is that the breakout or reaction from the zone is incredibly volatile and strong - this reaction should be clear and be obvious in relation to the recent candlestick sizes and price movements.

Often, as a rule of thumb, the stronger the reaction from a zone the more likely that a similar reaction will happen when the price reaches this zone again in the future.

- ### Quick Breakout

To become a good, valid zone the reaction from the zone touch should be close to instant if not straight away - with very little to no consolidation and market rest at the zone.

This is because the reaction from the market we want to see are presented due to influxes of orders from large financial institutions which rapidly change the buying/selling ratio and present a shift in market movement.

- ### Exact/Precise Zones

Another important defining factor of a supply/demand zone is that the repeating zone is very tight and the price reactions happen very close to one another in terms of price value.

If this occurs, it means the price zone is very narrow and therefore the price converts the buyer/seller ratio very quickly - as expected and so defines a valid supply/demand zone.

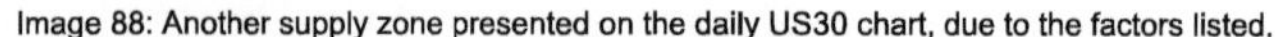
Image 88: Another supply zone presented on the daily US30 chart, due to the factors listed.

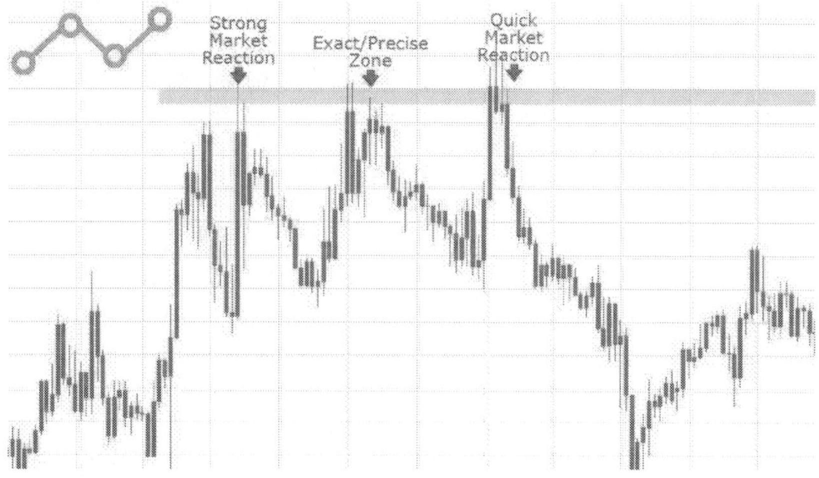

Traps & Fake-Outs

The idea of forex trading means that there are many profitable areas, be it a small retail trader, a broker or even large financial institution - one of these groups profit when the other two lose, and so these groups have different wishes in the financial market.

A financial broker profits when retail traders lose money on their positions - this is why you may have noticed that a trade with many confluence factors and a large expected win percentage reverses and moves in the completely wrong direction - this is because brokers actually have large power in the markets, and combined with large financial organisations ("whales") they create a trade with as many losers as possible which makes more profit for the brokers.

Indications of a trap

1. The price is moving consistently in one direction, with no strong impulses in the reverse direction. This was caught by some traders, but not many - and so the traders are now hoping for an entry into the trend either through a retest or swing change.

2. Once the price makes a new swing extreme (low or high) traders without positions will wait for this swing to break previous levels so that entries can be made.

3. The price then moves out of the range of the previous swing and is officially a new swing high/low. This creates a seemingly perfect entry for traders, and so many traders impatiently enter in the direction of the overall trend. This is supported by the

fact that many of these traps start with a very strong move in the direction of the trend.

4. The price then instantly reverses and “snaps” in the opposite direction - in one candlestick or less, and often with a market gap; professional traders quickly notice this and enter their positions in the direction of the reversal which only accelerates the end of the trend and swings quickly into new highs/lows.

5. This forces the traders that impatiently entered to be confused, with large losses and thinking that the “market is working against them” - whereas, if they were more educated and patient they could have avoided and entered in the correct direction.

Image 89: A bullish trap presented on the hourly New Zealand Dollar to Candian Dollar, with a reversal after a swing high.

Avoiding traps:

If you are constantly wary of entering a trade due to it possibly being a “trap” then your win percentage will increase incredibly - however you will also enter less trades, and this may not suit some styles of traders; even so it is impossible to avoid every trap the market throws at traders; but knowing about them can help.

Waiting for Confirmed Swings

A simple method of avoiding the majority of fake breaks and/or traps is by waiting for the candlesticks to form and close completely before entering a new positions - this means being patient until the candle closes outside of the previous swing ranges and ensures a larger win percentage - and such will create a better strategy in the longer term.

Refrain from Late Entries

As mentioned earlier, traps occur in a trend when the market has been moving consistently in one direction for a while and traders have not yet entered - this can be solved by entering earlier at the start of the longer term trend, or by avoiding entering entirely if you have realised that you will have a late entry - this once again tests the trader's patience and greed.

Image 90: A bearish trap displayed on the 4 hour Euro to Australian Dollar, that could have been avoided by being patient.

Format of Traps

The Vault Formation

The vault formation is an accompanying confluence factor to the opportunity of a fake breakout. The formation occurs when the price exits a prior trading range and presents either a weak breakout with little movement in the next multiple candles or a complete reversal in one candle through the production of a large candle wick - often this formation of a vault in one direction is a strong enough fakeout to cause large financial "whales" to flip the price basis and breakout in the other direction of the aforementioned trading range.

This vault formation should be taken as a very strong factor and can be used solely to base a trade for risk tolerant traders, or can be used in conjunction with other signals and confluence factors for more cautious traders.

Jonas Navardauskas
Owner of .4x Team

Image 91: A vault formation constructed on the daily US30 chart after failing a breakout.

Double Zone Retest Trap

A second retest at a major zone is a key area to watch and wait for traps/fake-breakouts, this is because the majority of other traders are excited and wait for the breakout of this zone to enter with a high risk:reward ratio in the direction of the supposed breakout and so often enter earlier than they should - before the confirmed breakout with a closed candle.

Image 92: A wick retest at a zone is rejected during an uptrend, and becomes a trap on the hourly gold (XAU/USD) chart.

Jonas Navardauskas
Owner of .4x Team

Compounding

In my belief, compounding correctly while trading any sort of financial instrument is incredibly important and separates the world's best traders from the rest. The results and possibilities available while taking perfect advantage of compounding is sometimes unbelievable - and so should be prioritised while learning trading as a beginner, or be developed as soon as possible as a skill for already profitable traders.

Compounding while trading as an idea is quite simple: by profiting, you have the ability to make larger amounts of money with the money you've just made.

This idea can be applied in two main ways, and a truly proficient trader should be able to take advantage of both.

Account Compounding

This method of compounding is the classic idea heard everywhere - on financial TV, news or even loan agreements.

In banking, this is referred to as compound interest - and the same principle can be applied to your trading account.

By maintaining the same lot sizes and risk value, despite your account increasing in equity due to profitable trades, you are missing out on a large percentage of potential profits. If a trader can appropriately adapt their lot sizes consistently upon each trade, and maintaining an appropriate risk management strategy, this same trader will see significantly better results in the long term.

In theory, you should double your lot size when your account equity doubles - meaning you're facing a similar level of risk and you can continue growing your account at a consistent pace, percentage wise. However, it is proven that the larger the account is, the less a trader is willing to risk and so they reduce their percentage risk until a level where they are happy with both profits and losses.

When taking advantage of account compounding, in the long term, it is vital to remain patient while your account is new and not radically increase lot sizes after a loss - to avoid emotional trading.

Many multi-millionaire traders have preached the severity of long term compounding, such as Warren Buffet saying that "nobody wants to get rich slowly" and Curtis M. Faith writing a book on the topic; titled "Way of the Turtle".

Image 93: A key chart representing the importance of compounding profits to earn significantly more over a span of time.

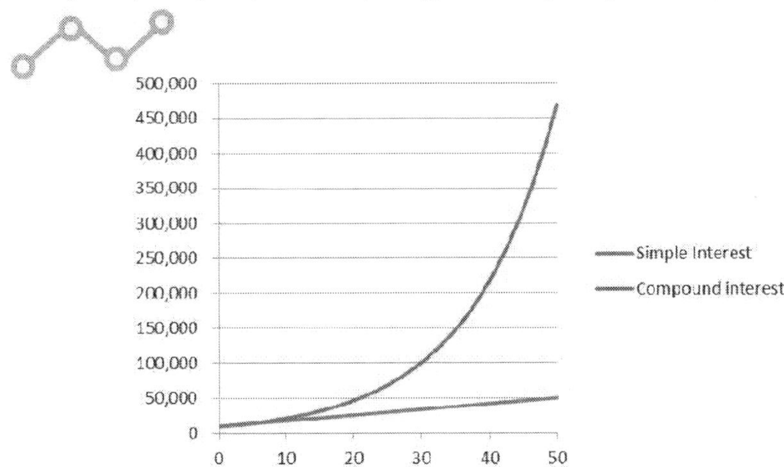

Trade Compounding

This method of compounding is significantly more important to practise, due to it being a lot more difficult to make correct use of.

In short, trade compounding is the idea of taking advantage of leveraging provided by brokers and over-leveraging a trade position once the market has started moving strongly with appropriate price action in the expected direction.

This strategy should be used mainly on accurate swing trades with many confluence factors. By entering with a usual lot size at your normal entry position, and maintaining it all the way to the take profit, you are securing an appropriate amount of profit compared to your risk.

Image 94: The original entry on the daily US30 chart, following a trend line retest and RSI Divergence.

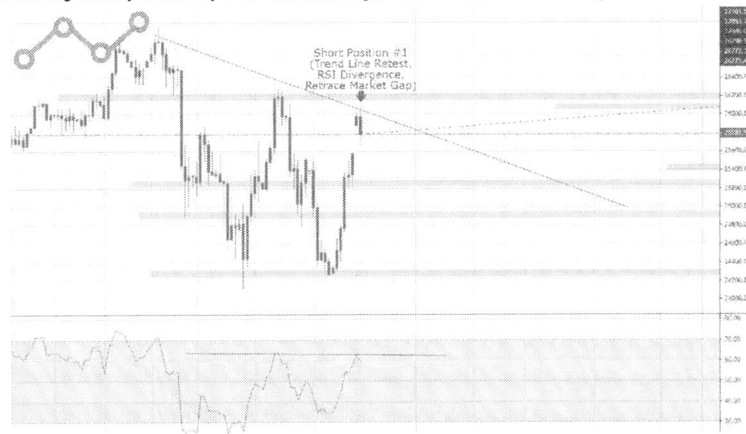

However, by moving down to the lower timeframes and searching for bullish or bearish continuation patterns (after the initial market impulse) you can enter a larger lot size with a very tight stop loss, as the price has a high chance of continuing the previous impulse - meaning you now have two trade positions opened in the same direction (one original small position, and another later but with a larger lot size), but both are set at breakeven stop losses.

Image 95: The second, larger entry on the US30 trade due to a consolidation between two zones and negative economic news.

In these situations, the larger lot size position is profiting significantly more than the original position, even though the price has moved less than from the original entry. This is an appropriate method of over-leveraging your account, as the price has already shown the expected market performance and you are just greatly amplifying your profit with a small amount of risk - due to the tight stop loss on the secondary position.

This trade compounding can be repeated each time the price prints an appropriate price action continuation pattern in the direction of your overall market analysis direction. Meaning that scaling up accounts and sometimes doubling, tripling or even quadrupling a small account in one trade is often possible.

Image 96: A third, final entry on the US30 trade following a break and retest of a support - amplified by a continuation pattern.

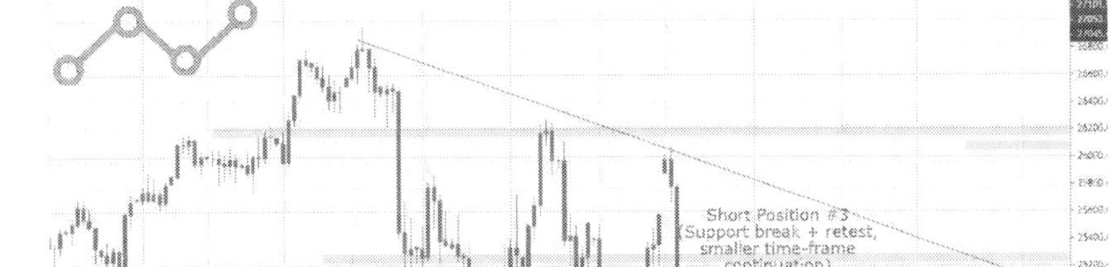

In the long run, by aggressively trade compounding and taking advantage of long term account compounding you will guarantee that you are maximising profits, as long as your trading ability is consistent and a streak of losing trades over a few days or weeks will not margin you out.

Image 97: All three trade positions are closed with large profit as market closes near a key support zone.

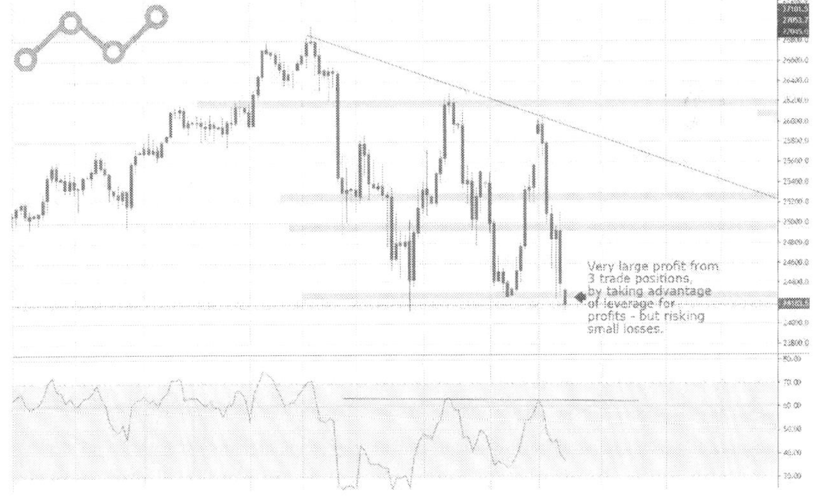

Jonas Navardauskas
Owner of .4x Team

Real Trading Account Case Study

€53.30 to €32,405.37 in 19 days

This account by Jonas is quite possibly the best example of compounding in the whole history of foreign exchange trading, and shows what can be achieved with perfect trading.

Following a deposit of €53.30, this account grew from €53.30 euros to €32,405.37 in a span of 8 trades in 19 days (of which only 6 days were spent trading) - trading only the US30 and XAUUSD (gold).

For the first 3 trading days, US30 was used to grow the account from small values into more respectable figures - in order to trade XAUUSD appropriately.

Due to XAUUSD often having stronger pullbacks and corrections than the US30, it is important to have a large account or to use very strong risk management to ensure your account does not get margined out.

Additionally, mastering one or a certain number of pairs is highly recommended - which can only be done when investing large amounts of time monitoring, backtesting and trading a certain currency pair.

This is what has been done with US30 and XAUUSD for us due to the volatile movements and breakouts they consist of; however, they are also greatly affected by economic news and extra care must be taken in case of sudden global emergencies or changes.

It is important to understand and learn the power of both trading and compounding.

This account grew by 60698.1% over 8 trades, in 6 days of trading - which trumps the earning potential and risk from scalping and many other methods of trading.

I hope that you can take advantage of this case study, and learn a significant amount - it should consolidate your knowledge learnt from this book and show you what can be achieved.

-

Jonas

2019/07/01 (+86 pips)

The first day of the account, the 1st of July, following the deposit of €53.30.
Starting Balance: €53.30 | Ending Balance: €137.87

Image 98 and 99: TradingView analysis and MetaTrader 4 trade confirmation for 2019/07/01.

The US30 daily presented a possible resistance rejection, and so the first trade was a sell from 26750 to 26664, due to previous price action moving similar to this.

With very small accounts such as this, using tight stop losses is not advised - you should be content and know the fact that if your analysis is wrong, then your account will margin out. This is because many traders lose their accounts after many small losses, due to not allowing their trades to breathe and attempting to be correct about unrealistic risk to reward ratio trades.

It is better to allow your trade to breathe and understanding that is it is very rare to get an exact perfect entry.

Similarly, the trade was not a large swing, as securing profit and growing percentages should be priorities when compounding very small accounts - it is important to care more about the chance of success of the trade, rather than the risk to reward ratio if you are multiplying accounts.

Using a 1.0 lot is unadvised on such a small account, as having almost any drawdown will margin your account out; however, as mentioned previously we are content with risking this account in case our analysis is incorrect.

2019/07/05 (+187 pips)

The second trade of the account was placed on the 5th of July.
Starting Balance: €137.87 | Ending Balance: €395.04

Image 100 and 101: TradingView analysis and Metatrader 4 trade confirmation for 2019/07/05.

The US30 once again presented a rejection - this time from the ascending trend line, and the sell position was placed from 26993 to around 26806, and another compound entry was placed from 26958 to around 26806.

This trade is a great example of both account compounding and trade compounding, both of which are covered in chapters previous in this book.

By nearly multiplying the account by 300% in the first trade, it is possible to enter trades a bit later for an increased success percentage - because with more free margin, you are able to withstand larger pullbacks.

Entering once early at 26993 upon the first signs of rejection allows you enter quite early to ensure you do not miss the majority of the market movements - and then waiting for a lower time frame continuation pattern to enter another additional position.

This happened at 26958, and therefore another short position was entered - this ensures profit maximisation, as you are using very large lot sizes for your account size with the low risk created due to the pair already showing expected movement signs.

2019/07/08 (+175 pips)

On the third day of trading, one trade was placed on the 8th of July.
Starting Balance: €395.04 | Ending Balance: €510.44

Image 102 & 103: TradingView analysis and Metatrader 4 confirmation for 2019/07/08.

The US30 continued it's rejection from the ascending trend line from the prior trades, and so new compound entries were made, with entries at 26932 taking profit at around 26815.

As explained earlier, due to the growth of the account, it is appropriate to begin increasing lots even at the original position - and not just later on after seeing bearish continuation patterns forming.

While this account is still relatively small, it is important to secure profits and ensure that you are maximising the money made from each position - unlike a large account where you would be using 2% risk, and can allow the trade to run into drawdown for a while without worrying.

These positions were taken due to the expected bearish movement continuing, and essentially made these positions range trades - between the ascending trend line and prior supports. This is quite a simple strategy and can be entered multiple times, due to range trades taking place at both ends, and repeating each time the price retests a zone.

2019/07/17 (+81 pips)

On the fourth day of trading, market opportunities were spotted on the 17th of July.
Starting Balance: €510.44 | Ending Balance: €1,099.45

Image 104 & 105: TradingView analysis and Metatrader 4 confirmation for 2019/07/17.

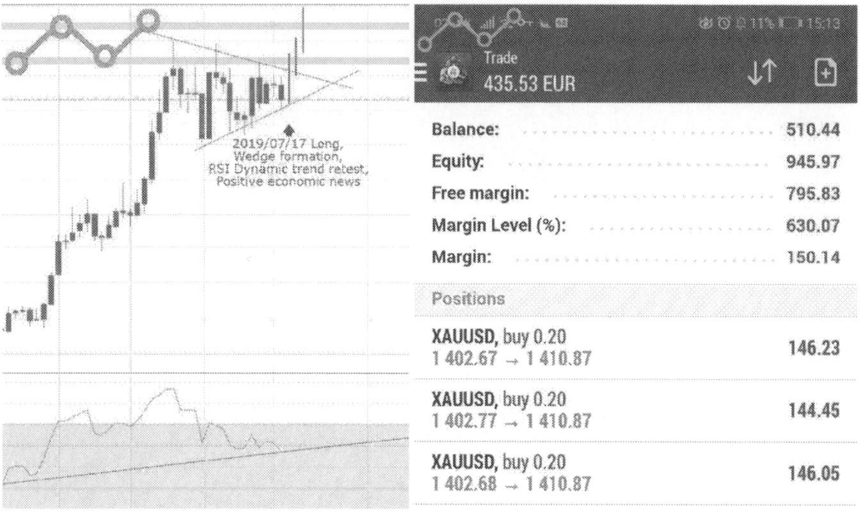

Following the previous market analysis on US30, there was a change of market structure as the market did not continue past the ascending trend line - forming a market wedge that will feature a volatile market movement in either the bullish or bearish direction.

Due to the RSI dynamic trend line retest, and the prior market impulse being bullish - it could also be seen that this wedge is a form of market correction before the next bullish impulse.

Because of these reasons, three new long positions were taken in anticipation for the bullish breakthrough - this analysis was correct and the positions from the 1402 area were closed with profit at around 1410.87 for a total of ~80 pips.

Despite the importance of trade compounding, there was not any appropriate continuation patterns present after the initial breakthrough, and so profit was only made from the original positions. At this point, after securing profit it is incredibly important to monitor the price action in this area - as many other traders may have spotted this breakout and decisions made by large financial institutions (whales) might affect the original analysis; creating a fakeout.

Jonas Navardauskas
Owner of .4x Team

2019/07/18 (+167 pips)

On the 18th of July, 3 trades were opened, with the final trade being closed the following day.
Starting Balance: €1,099.45 | Ending Balance: €7,529.89

Image 106, 107, 108 & 109: TradingView analysis and Metatrader 4 confirmation for 2019/07/18.

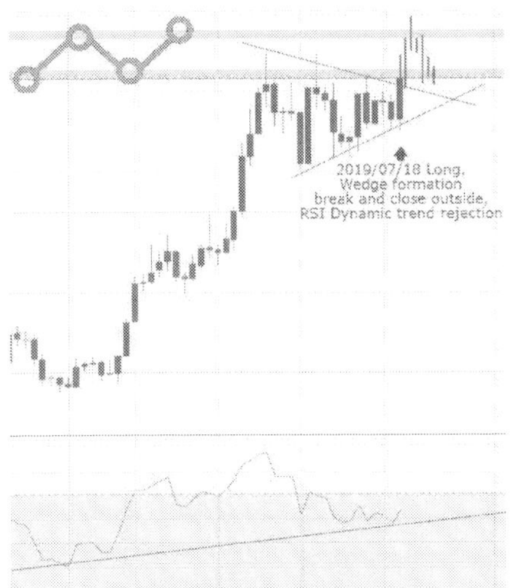

Trade
934.83 EUR

Balance:	1 099.45
Equity:	2 034.28
Free margin:	1 324.57
Margin Level (%):	286.63
Margin:	709.71

Positions

XAUUSD, buy 0.40 1 422.95 → 1 425.66	96.57
XAUUSD, buy 0.40 1 422.94 → 1 425.66	96.93
XAUUSD, buy 0.40 1 422.35 → 1 425.66	117.95
XAUUSD, buy 0.40 1 420.96 → 1 425.66	166.78
XAUUSD, buy 0.40 1 421.28 → 1 425.66	156.09
XAUUSD, buy 0.40 1 421.36 → 1 425.66	153.59
XAUUSD, buy 0.40 1 421.38 → 1 425.66	152.52

Trade
4 869.44 EUR

Balance:	2 081.56
Equity:	6 951.00
Free margin:	4 148.34
Margin Level (%):	248.01
Margin:	2 802.66

Positions

XAUUSD, buy 0.50 1 438.50 → 1 438.57	3.11
XAUUSD, buy 0.50 1 438.47 → 1 438.57	4.44
XAUUSD, buy 0.50 1 438.47 → 1 438.57	4.44
XAUUSD, buy 0.50 1 438.37 → 1 438.57	8.87
XAUUSD, buy 0.50 1 438.20 → 1 438.57	16.42
XAUUSD, buy 0.50 1 434.74 → 1 438.57	169.92
XAUUSD, buy 0.50 1 434.94 → 1 438.57	161.05
XAUUSD, buy 0.50 1 435.11 → 1 438.57	153.51
XAUUSD, buy 0.50 1 435.12 → 1 438.57	153.06

Trade
426.51 EUR

Balance:	7 403.61
Equity:	7 830.12
Free margin:	7 190.45
Margin Level (%):	1224.09
Margin:	639.67

Positions

XAUUSD, buy 2.50 1 438.35 → 1 440.29	431.51

Jonas Navardauskas
Owner of .4x Team

After monitoring the price action the previous day of XAUUSD, and noticing that the daily candle had closed entirely without any wicks - this presented highly overpowering bullish momentum, and allowed us to continue with our long positions from the original analysis.

By firstly entering upon the break at the 1421 area, and monitoring the price action - it was important to understand that consolidation can reverse the trend quickly after a sudden bullish rally, such as the one that we had anticipated.

And so, because of this possibility, settling for ~30 pips was the appropriate measure to take for the first trade. It is possible that significantly more profit could have been made, but due to very large lot sizes being used in relation to the account size, any drawdown is worrying and could margin the account out.

This meant that the first positions opened were closed with profit at around 1425.66 and once again monitoring the market movements was key to finding new positions, ideally after a lower time frame continuation pattern or breakout.

This is what happened later on in the day, when the price had reached the 1426 region and new bullish entries were taken - this market momentum continued incredibly strongly, accelerated by negative economic news increasing the demand for gold as a stable currency form. By aggressively trade compounding, around 20 compound positions were opened as gold maintained its bullish rally - greatly amplifying the account value without risking a significant amount. All of these compound positions were closed later at around 1439 - for a 116 pip profit from the original positions.

Following these profitable trades, a final position was opened prior to the evening which was closed early the next day - from 1438.35 to profit taken at around 1440.29, for a pip profit of ~20.

All of these opened trades resulted in a 167 pip profit for the 18th of July, similar to the 187 pip profit on the 5th of July.

But due to aggressive account compounding and trade compounding, instead of profiting €257.17 from 187 pips, the positions taken this day resulted in €6,430 profit from only 167 pips.

2019/07/19 (+182 pips)

Video and proof of this final trade is available on the home page of www.4xteam.co.uk
On the final day of trading, one trade was taken on the 19th of July.
Starting Balance: €7,529.89 | Ending Balance: €32,405.37

Image 110 & 111: TradingView analysis and Metatrader 4 confirmation for 2019/07/19.

With the best positions taken at 1438.69, a rejection from the 70 RSI level forecasted a bearish sell-off following the bullish market breakout at a prior resistance.

With the expected market movement and volatility following the RSI key area rejection, it was important to compound positions aggressively to maximise the profit in this market sell-off.

At each small market consolidation region, a new position was taken, as the floating profit from the previous positions will be able to cover any small drawdown during the consolidation period - however, due to the overall market sentiment being bearish from the higher time-frame analysis; we were confident in the new positions.

Not all positions are visible in the screenshot, and a video proving that this is a live account, with the remaining positions on this final trade can be found on www.4xteam.co.uk.

Example Setups

Previous Trades

EUR/NZD 03.06.19 (+650 pips)

On the daily timeframe, the euro to new zealand dollar presented a clear break of the ascending trend line caused by a clean price rejection from a previous supply level/resistance zone at the psychological level of 1.72 and promptly reversed.

Following the breakout, there is an exact retest at 1.71 and multiple pin bar price action candlestick signals to confirm the sell-off is about to begin.

The trader enters the trade at 1.71047 with a tight stop loss of 1.71566 just above the previous pin bar highs, and a large target of 1.64548. This presents a risk reward of 1:17.4 and provides many confirmation signals to enter the trade with a small stop loss and compound if the trade continues in the desired direction.

One main aspect that cannot be overlooked is how close the stop loss has been placed. Large financial institutions and banks may try to “stop-hunt” the smaller traders right above 1.72 so a trader must be wary of this and adjust stop loss as needed if a bullish rally begins to develop.

This trade continued its bearish momentum and ended up closing at take profit, resulting in a 650 pip profit.

GBP/CHF 03.06.19 (+241 pips)

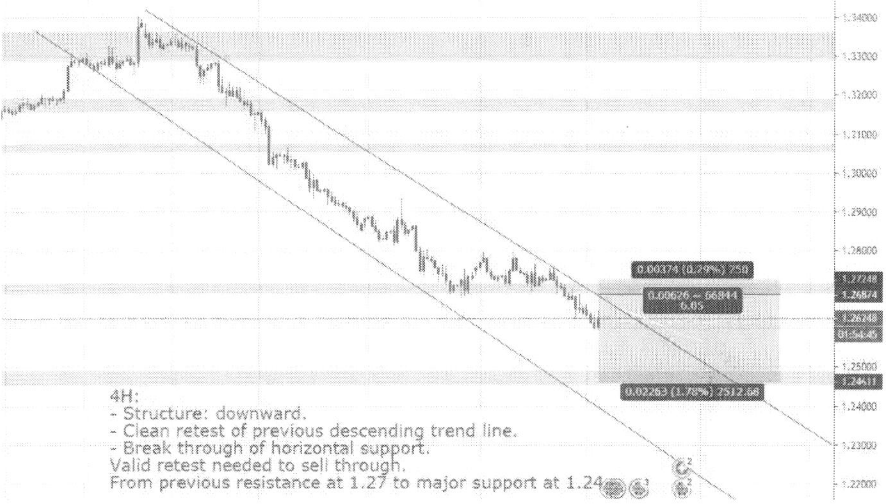

On the 4 hour and daily timeframe, the pound to swiss franc presented a clear retest of the descending trend line, this is caused by a price rejection of the psychological level of 1.28 which continues to act as a Support/Resistance flip zone.

Prior to this controlled breakout, there was a bearish pennant forming in between the 1.28 and 1.27 figures which resulted in a moderate sell off - as a trader you face two options: being an aggressive trader, and entering the trade instantly after the breakout. This will often increase the risk:reward ratio of a trade, but will reduce the hit rate due to possible pullbacks.

If you are a more reserved trader, and our preferred trading style - we often recommend a valid retest to the zone to act as a flip zone. This is what appeared after the initial breakout bearish candle and appeared as a pin bar - from which we would enter with a significantly tighter stop loss and therefore a greater risk reward ratio.

This trade showed valid movement and momentum, and ended up entering at the price 1.26874 and taking profit at 1.24611 resulting in a 241 pip profit.

EUR/NZD 05.05.19 (+555 pips)

On the 4 hour timeframe, the euro to new zealand dollar had printed a clear supply zone at the 1.695 price level, making the price fall heavily and drastically. This market movement was opposite to the general market direction as presented by the two upward moving averages, which have been respected as dynamic support and resistance levels prior.

The market then reaches a similar level to this once again, which can be accepted due to the idea of support and resistance being zones and not exact prices. Following an appropriate market rejection and shift in market direction after the second market peak, the trader looks for a bullish trade position, as it will be more forgiving when trading in the direction of the market.

The market price then continued to fall to 1.68638, and the trader enters a long position upon seeing rejection at the moving averages, because it has already been decided that they can be used as dynamic support and resistance due to previous price action.

This trade resulted in a close at 1.74189 at the end of the market trading week on Friday, for a total profit of 555 pips.

NZD/USD 12.05.19 (+104 pips)

On the 4 hour timeframe, the New Zealand dollar to US dollar had presented a strong, volatile bullish market movement after printing clear price action rejection at the psychological market level of 0.66. Following this, the market continued its bullish rally up to the moving averages as dynamic support and resistance levels - from which it began to reverse and continue the overall bearish market trend.

Upon reaching the 0.66 demand level once again, many traders were searching for a bullish trade position, and many entered too early without seeing any appropriate price action. The market did not continue upwards, and instead many of the traders who were in a long position were forced to close out their trades. As explained earlier (the closing of positions, in theory, opens a new position in the opposite direction) amplified the bearish market movement and printed an extreme pin bar.

The trader, after seeing all of this, should be wary of entering a bullish position as it could just be another market fake-out. Instead, the trader should have a bearish bias towards the market, due to the overall negative market trend.

With the price being at a key support/resistance flip zone of the previously mentioned 0.66 psychological level, and a clear market rejection from the dynamic moving average resistance; the trader can then enter a bearish position at the price of 0.65967 and maintain this trade until market closure on Friday, where the trade was closed at the price of 0.64920 for an overall profit of 104 pips.

XAU/USD 19.05.19 (+272 pips)

On the daily timeframe, the gold chart had printed a clear descending channel limited by a trend line connecting all of the previous market swing highs. Often, in a downwards channel, the previous market swing's support acts as the next swing's resistance and vice versa in an ascending channel. This means that by accurately displaying your support and resistance flip zones, you are more likely to recognise valid rejections and take advantage of them.

In this trade, the price showed an appropriate bearish market movement on the daily time-frame from a support/resistance flip zone. As gold is in a downwards structure and overall trend, the trader can enter a bearish position with a close stop loss above the high of this daily candle.

The trader enters at the price of 1297.03, and holds the trade until the price continues past the next major support level, and instead hits the bottom of the descending channel. This was achieved by the end of the trading week and was closed at 1269.78, meaning an overall profit of 272 pips.

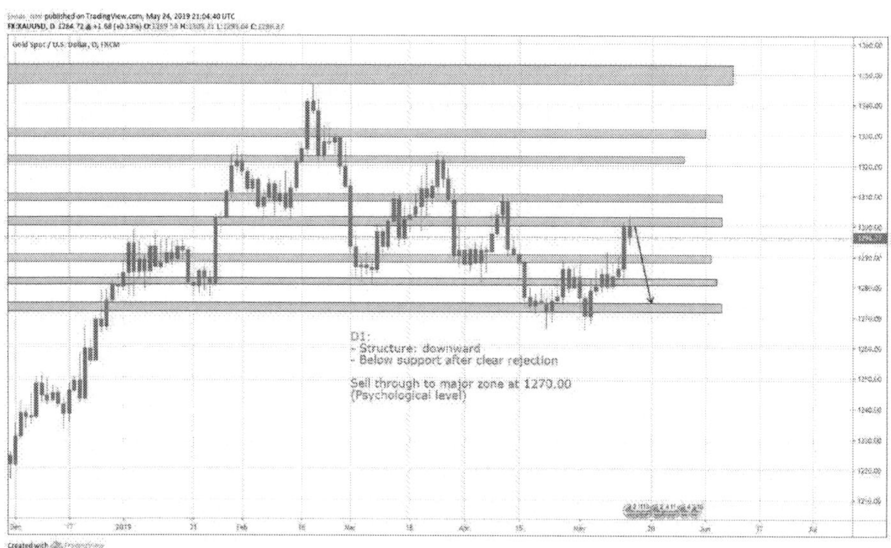

GBP/CHF 02.06.19 (+77 pips)

On the daily timeframe, the British pound to Swiss franc was positioned in a strong bearish rally and was breaking through many trend lines and supports - by most chance due to important economic news or decisions made by financial whales.

When seeing a situation similar to this, it is important to wait for a corrective period and then enter if appropriate price action has been presented - it is not recommended to enter instantly in the direction of the market impulse; because a volatile rally in one direction is often followed by the same volatility rally or even stronger in the opposite direction.

Therefore, after seeing the heavy drop of over 600 pips, we waited for a correction following the original impulse, and as expected the 1.28 psychological level acted as a resistance from a past market swings support - this was a key level and was unlikely to be broken.

Similarly, the price broke out of the descending wedge and the only main resistance soon was at 1.24 - this encourages the trader to enter at the price of 1.26384 with a tight stop loss of 1.27 and a goal of 1.24, resulting in a great risk to reward ratio of 1:3.84.

Unfortunately, this trade did not prove a lot of market movement - possibly due to exhaustion caused by the high momentum rally taking place in the week prior, and instead profit was taken at 1.25612 - resulting in a 77 pip profit.

USD/CAD 09.06.19 (+201 pips)

On the daily timeframe, the US Dollar to Canadian Dollar was continually retracting to the ascending trend line forming a clean upwards channel and creating an overall uptrend.

However, on a larger time frame such as the weekly, this ascending channel forms a correction from the original impulse that was created by the crash from the 1.37 region to the 1.325 area. This accentuates the importance of following a top down analysis - as you now know that it is more important to have a bearish bias towards the market to try and catch the next market impulse.

After deciding the initial market bias from your top down analysis, this break of the corrective structure on the daily timeframe should be regarded highly, as it represents the start of the long term market impulse. Following the strong breakout of the trend line, combined with the break of the daily support at 1.335; the trader can enter a short position at the price of 1.32683 with a stop loss right above the previous support at 1.335 and a target of 1.3 as the target.

This trade presented an appropriate 1:3.27 risk reward ratio, but was a likely trade due to the initial bias being based on a very high timeframe analysis. This trade resulted profit taken at 1.30673 meaning a 201 overall pip profit.

EUR/USD 16.06.19 (+233 pips)

On the daily timeframe, the euro to US Dollar was partaking in a bearish descending channel, following clean rejections at the upper descending trend line and appropriate price action at each touch. The price then began to stall at the support zone, but continual downside pressure forced the price into a descending wedge, where a breakout of either direction is imminent.

It is not advised to enter for these breakouts as they are often catalysed by economic news or other unpredictable situations, therefore as a patient trader it is significantly better to wait for the breakout and trade corrective movements afterwards.

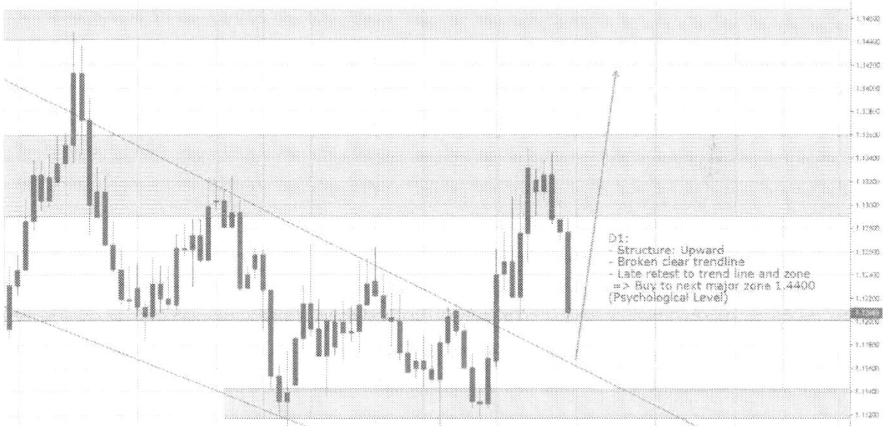

In this trade, after having broken out of the channel, a zone retest was presented but the trade was not taken as the retest did not touch the trend line, but instead a support resistance flip zone. Depending on your personal risk tolerance, it is possible to have entered the trade upon the first retest and respectable profit could have been made.

However, it is recommended to wait and see an actual retest at the trend line combined with a rejection from the major support at the 1.114 area. This introduces more, strong confluence factors and encourages us to enter a long position at a price of 1.11812. This trade was later closed at a price of 1.14142 for an overall profit of 233 pips.

Jonas Navardauskas
Owner of .4x Team

NZD/CAD 23.06.19 (+132 pips)

On the daily timeframe, the New Zealand dollar to Canadian Dollar was moving in a descending channel, with respecting price action presented at each trend line touch - and short positions can be taken at each market swing high, depending on the traders risk tolerance.

We personally waited for a wedge formation, which was presented on the chart with a previous swing's support being the same support for the next market swing - suggesting a shift in market conditions.

By being presented with clear price action confluence and a shift in market conditions, we were confident in the chance that a correction of the previous market impulse (presented in the bearish rally from the 0.89 area to the 0.86 region) will continue up to the last minor resistance at the psychological level of 0.88; which would also correspond with the descending trend line.

Generally, it is not advised to trade for market corrections and instead analysis should be restrained to entering into impulses as they will be more forgiving - however, due to the many confluence factors we entered and profited off the correction.

Entering at a price of 0.86688 our take profit of 0.88 was hit within three days, resulting in a 132 pip profit.

Jonas Navardauskas
Owner of .4x Team

XAU/USD 30.06.19 (+266 pips)

On the daily timeframe, the gold chart (XAUUSD) presented a descending channel, which was eventually broken out of with a strong bullish rally.

It is preferred to wait for a market retest of the descending trend line upon a break similar to this; however, that did not happen and so no trade positions were taken. Instead, it is appropriate to wait for the price to reach a market zone that has been tested before and has caused a respectable market reaction.

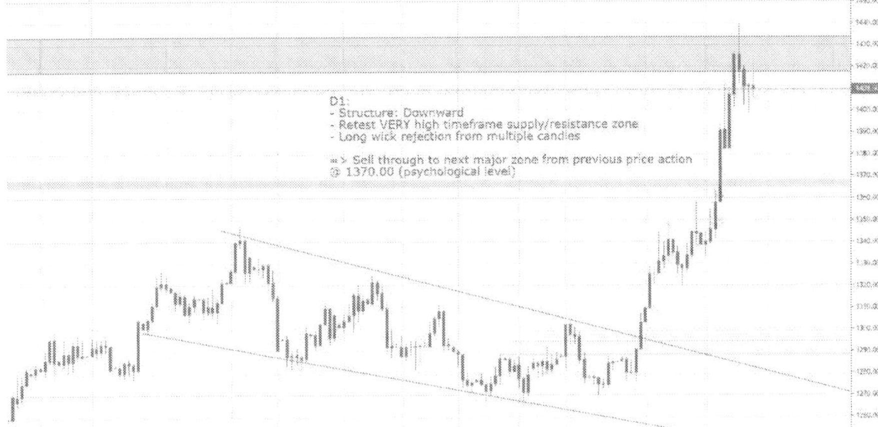

Finally, as expected, the market continued its bullish rally to the next major resistance zone, and provided clear price action confluence for a rejection trade. The candle wick presented on a daily time frame is often more than enough confirmation, as it presents a heavy market bias reversal over a whole day of market movement. This, complemented by a second candle wick in the zone 2 days later, prompts us to enter the trade at the price of 1409.50.

Trades similar to this are often recommended to enter, as they provide a clear invalidation level that can be used as a stop loss level. In this example, the stop loss was placed slightly above the resistance zone - as at that point, it is likely that the market has reacted to strong economic news and another breakout is expected.

By the end of the trading week, the market had sold off to a level of 1382.81 where profit was taken resulting in 266 pips.

Jonas Navardauskas
Owner of .4x Team

US30 07.07.2019 (+240 pips)

On the weekly timeframe, the US30 chart was displaying a large amount of volatility in both bullish rallies and bearish sell-offs.

This is a fantastic method of catching respectable amounts of pips, as it could be considered as a range trade - which happen between both areas of the range, and happen multiple times before they break down creating many trading opportunities.

Similarly, it is important to take advantage of clearly trending markets - as it is often easier to profit off of them than swinging markets that tend to consolidate after reaching certain market prices. In this trade the chart shows that as the market sentiment changes suddenly from bullish to bearish (or vice-versa) and it continues in that market direction for some time.

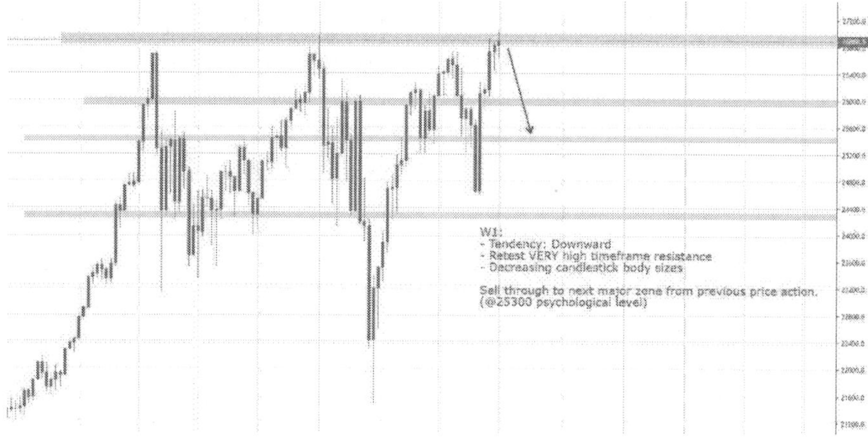

By providing a clear price action market slow down in the last few candlesticks prior to the trade entry, and being complemented by the candlestick wick rejection from the previous resistance zone - it was clear to enter a short position from the price 26888.5 and target previous minor support and psychological levels such as 26600.

As mentioned in other trade breakdowns, entering rejection trades provides great risk to reward ratios, as if the price continued past the major resistance then the analysis is invalidated and new market opportunities need to be found.

By the end of the trading week, the market had shown slow movement towards the downside and so profit was taken at the 26648.4 price instead of the 26600 target for a profit of 240 pips.

Jonas Navardauskas
Owner of .4x Team

CAD/JPY 13.07.2019 (+61 pips)

On the 4 hour timeframe, the Canadian Dollar to Japanese Yen printed clear movement between the two ascending trend line creating an ascending channel.

By entering at key areas near the trend lines it is possible to enter highly profitable positions with great risk to reward ratios, as the stop loss should not be placed far away - due to a quick reversal expected once a rejection from the price level is seen. This; however, should not be the only reasoning behind a trade and instead it is recommended to wait for possible confluence factors such as price action confirmation or lower timeframe patterns before entering a trade.

With the trader noticing the clear rejection from the upper ascending trend line, an overall bearish market bias should be taken despite the upwards trend. This is only due to the use of a comparatively low timeframe of 4 hours.

After deciding the trading bias, trading opportunities can be spotted after noticing that the price has formed a double top from the key psychological level 83.2 with clear downwards momentum after the most recent touch - this idea is also significantly complemented by a similar reaction from a similar price level long ago, on the left side of the trade example.

The trader therefore enters at a price of 82.811 after the final confirmation of a break of a minor support at the 82.9 level. This trade consolidated and did not show strong market momentum or volatility, but continued a general bearish market sentiment and continued down to 82.198 where profit was taken, due to it reaching the lower ascending trend line.

This trade therefore resulted in a 61 pip profit - but more importantly the price had finally reached the bottom of the ascending channel and the trading bias can be shifted to bullish; creating more lucrative trading opportunities in the near future for this pair.

Jonas Navardauskas
Owner of .4x Team

GBP/USD 20.07.2019 (+31 pips)

On the weekly timeframe, the Great Britain pound to US Dollar had displayed a strong downtrend after printing clear price action confluence from a prior key resistance zone. This market sell-off continued strongly, until a clear candle wick rejection was presented after reaching the ascending trend line.

Key zones such as the ascending trend line should be monitored very heavily, due to the large number of possible trading opportunities that could be presented; such as rejections, breakouts or range trades. In this scenario, the fact that the price had printed a clean rejection a few weeks prior, could also make the zone a demand zone due to the quick and strong reactions from this price level.

With the trader noticing the long consolidation period along the demand zone, strong market momentum can be expected in the future - this is accompanied by the clear price action confluence rejecting the trend line.

The trader therefore enters the trade at a price of 1.24975, and a close stop loss below the previous candlestick wicks at the psychological level of 1.24.

Unfortunately, the trade did continue consolidating and instead profit was taken at the 1.25290 price due to a lack of market reaction. It is important to be in a good position for strong economic events that could change the overall market sentiment, and so new trading positions will start being found when the price actually prints a rejection or a breakout.

Overall, this trade resulted in a 31 pip profit - which is unfortunately quite underwhelming for a trade based on the weekly timeframe; however, as mentioned previously, the market is not always perfect and reasonable decisions have to be made when the market is not moving as expected.

XAU/USD 27.07.2019 (+310 pips)

On the hourly time frame, the gold (XAU/USD) chart broke and retraced to a previous demand zone at the key psychological level of 1412.50 and rejected appropriately - rallying ~375 pips in the span of 9 hours.

The price then continued to fall through to the key level of 1412.50 and showed clear rejection signs twice - but with no volatile rally to follow. This means that an appropriate strong rejection is yet to happen, and requires the price to break a bit further past the support zone to allow a larger number of traders to enter in the bullish direction.

This is exactly what happened, and the price once again began a slow uptrend - with large candle wicks in both directions; meaning indecision between traders and as mentioned previously, consolidation similar to this indicates large momentum imminent.

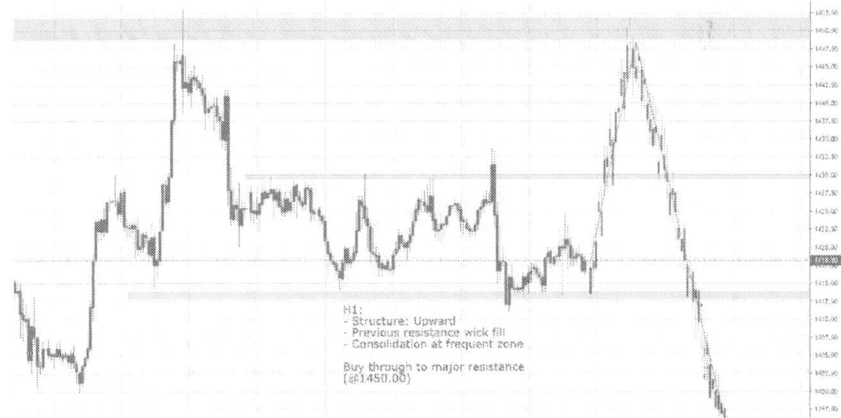

As the price was close to (but above a key support/demand zone), it was indicative that the price would break through in the bullish direction when appropriate market volume was introduced, instead of a bearish sell-off.

Therefore, the trader enters at the price of 1418.20 and a strong market rally pushed the price past all previous resistance zones towards the key 1450.00 psychological level.

With gold being such a volatile currency pair, that is heavily affected by news, economic events and other publications - it is important to be content with profits taken at range extremes; instead of trading for new market highs or lows.

This meant that profit was taken 1449.25 for a profit of 310 pips, and the pair was monitored heavily for a sign of rejection; for an entry in the bearish direction - possibly replicating the previous price action presented the last time the price reached this 1450.00 key level.

Jonas Navardauskas
Owner of .4x Team

USOIL 17.08.2019 (+612 pips)

On the daily timeframe, the USOIL chart was moving consistently in a downwards channel - with clear price action rejections at each descending trend line touch. Also, the market swing and duration is visibly more bearish, due to the downwards market movements being stronger, yet shorter than the upwards rallies.

However, there has been a noticeable formation of a demand zone at the key 50.00 psychological level - with a strong candlestick wick price fill on the most recent market swing. Due to this, it is vital to keep monitoring the price at this level, as a descending wedge should form relatively soon if both the descending channel and demand zone maintain their strength. This is what should be kept in mind when finding trade positions, as a trader does not want to be caught out by a volatile movement caused by the wedge.

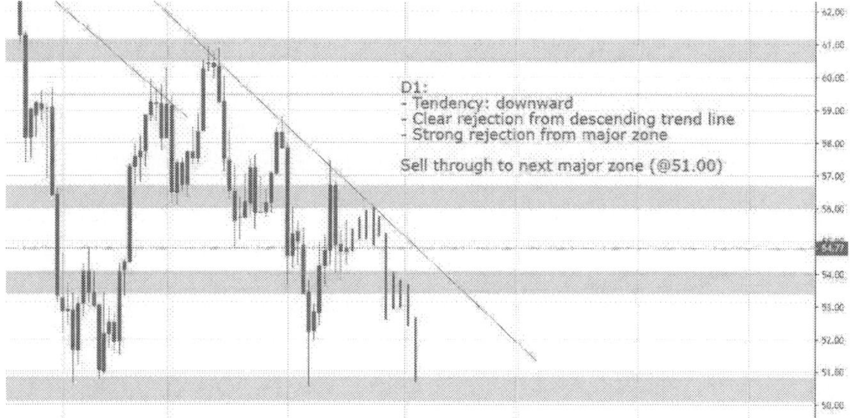

After noticing the key rejection from the descending trend line, a likely continuation of the price towards the 50.00 previous demand zone is expected after the next market high - which will happen at the next retest of the descending channel or previous resistance at the 57.00 price level.

Because of this analysis, the trader enters a long position at the price of 54.76 with intentions of a 57.00 take profit - to then later enter a short position, due to the overall bearish bias on USOIL.

Profit from the original position was taken at 57.09 - after noticing price action confluence indicating a reversal. These market conditions signalled for a short position from 57.09. The market reached new swing lows by the end of the trading week, and profit was taken at the price of 53.30 for an overall profit of 612 pips over the two trades.

US30 14.09.2019 (+298 pips)

On the daily timeframe, the US30 chart had a general bullish market sentiment as seen by the ascending trend line that has been respected accurately. It is key to perform a top down analysis while trading, meaning you move down in terms of time-frame length and mark key zones appropriately, to help you understand the market bias.

In terms of this trade, it was clear on both the monthly and weekly timeframe that the market is reaching a swing high at a resistance zone - and so the overall market sentiment is clearly bearish. This means that when moving down to the lower time-frames to find a market entry position, your position should be bearish to ensure the highest possible chance of success.

However; as mentioned previously, the US30 is heavily reactive to economic news and in cases such as the US & Iran tensions in early 2020, market support and resistance zones can often be ignored as the price will not respect them as expected.

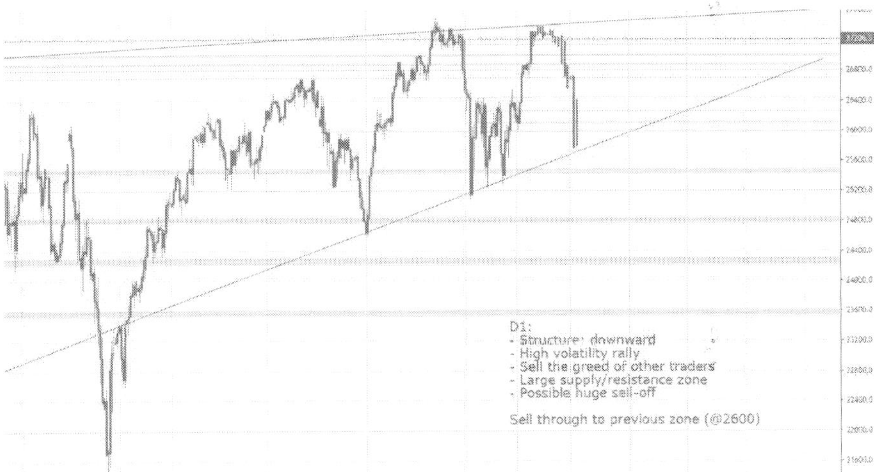

In this trading scenario; due to all of the aforementioned factors, such as the generally downwards structure decided after the top down analysis - complemented by the resistance zone at the 27200 psychological level, where the price is consolidating. The trader can enter this trade at the price of 27206.5 with long term intentions of a market sell-off towards the ascending trend line at the price of 25750.

At the start of the trading week, the market showed appropriate market momentum towards the downside, but had slowed down and started to consolidate by the end of the week - meaning that profit was taken at 26909.0 for a profit of 298 pips.

The market did, in fact, continue to the downside and reached the long term target at the price 25768.0 15 days later.

Jonas Navardauskas
Owner of .4x Team

XAU/USD 28.09.2019 (+1126 pips)

On the 4 hour timeframe, the gold (XAU/USD) chart had printed a descending trend line, confirmed by the general bearish down-trend on the higher time-frames - meaning that the overall long term trade sentiment should be downwards. This; however, does mean that you can still analyse and plan a trade in the bullish direction for the short term - to then get a better entry price for the larger, bearish position in the near future.

In this scenario, the price was clearly reaching a support level at the psychological 1490 price zone but continued its bearish selling pressure from the descending trend line. This creates a typical descending wedge, indicating strong imminent momentum in either the bullish or bearish direction. However, due to the price not being trapped by the trend line, it is highly likely that the price will continue upwards - towards the descending trend line or even to the previous resistance, despite the general bearish market sentiment.

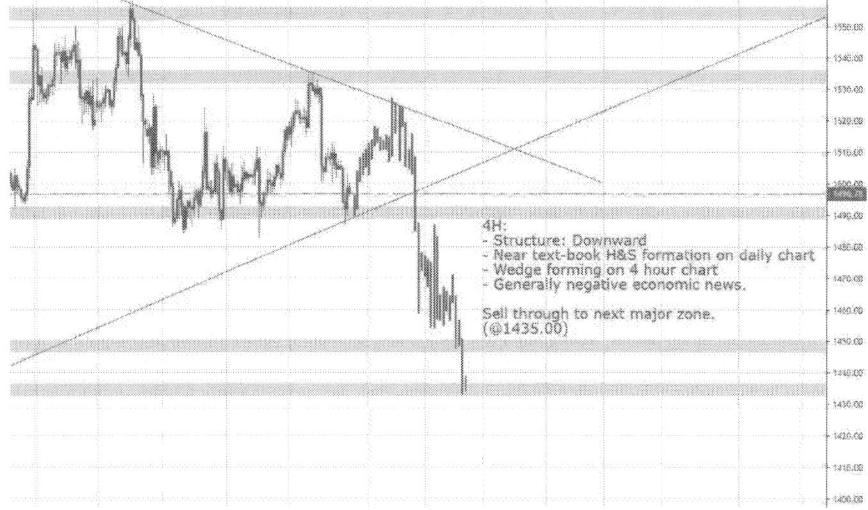

Due to this analysis, the trader can enter a long position towards a trend line or resistance retest. This means that an entry was taken at the 1496.78 price with a goal of around the 1530 region - and if the price shows appropriate rejection later then a bearish position can be considered.

This is exactly what happened with the XAU/USD market - by printing a clear price action candle wick up to 1534.93, profit was taken from the long position and a short position was entered with a long term target of 1450, due the possibility of a descending wedge breakout.

The market then broke out of the descending wedge, and began to consolidate at 1460.42, where profit was taken for an overall profit of 1126 pips in these two trades.

Jonas Navardauskas
Owner of .4x Team

NAS100 05.10.2019 (+509 pips)

On the 4 hour timeframe, the NAS100 chart was in a clear bearish trend, following a key market swing high after being rejected from the higher time-frame descending trend line, twice. This creates a similar trade scenario to the previous XAU/USD trade on the 28.09.2019, where a wedge formation is expected to happen - but the bullish and bearish price pressure is not close enough to cause a breakout.

Therefore, in this scenario it is key to wait for a better bullish trade position upon the formation of the wedge, or to enter a bearish short position early in anticipation of the formation. This depends on your personal risk tolerance as a trader. However, due to the generally downward market sentiment decided by our top down analysis - we were confident in the downward continuation towards the ascending trend line.

In this trade, we entered at the price 7749.4 in favour of the downside (because of the approach to both the steeper descending trend line and a possible support/resistance flip zone) with targets of the ascending trend line at the 7560 price region, to then get a great bullish entry for the breakout of the wedge.

The NAS continued downwards towards our target, and profit from the first position was taken at 7565.3 - where we entered a long position for a strong market reaction towards the long term descending trend line as shown in the image.

As expected, the NAS broke out of the wedge in the bullish direction and showed great momentum towards our target - meaning that the trade position was closed at 7890 - where the market consolidated due to finally having reached the trend line.

Jonas Navardauskas
Owner of .4x Team

Conclusion

I would like to take a moment to thank you for purchasing and reading the .4x Trader's Manual, and hope that you have taken advantage of all the education included in it.

Now it is time to begin using your newly learned concepts and techniques - be it from technical analysis, to risk management or even compounding to amplify your trading ability and succeed in the market.

Please feel free to contact a member of the .4xTeam for any inquires in the appropriate channel:

Jonas:

- Instagram (*@jonas.4xteam*)
- Email (*jonas@4xteam.co.uk*)

Trading Team:

- Email (*traders@4xteam.co.uk*)

PR Personnel:

- Email (*publicrelations@4xteam.co.uk*)

As mentioned before, I wish you the best of luck in trading all kinds of financial instruments - and am excited to hear about your success in the future, through email or social media.

- Jonas

Printed in Germany
by Amazon Distribution
GmbH, Leipzig